WHEN SCHOOLDAYS WERE FUN

WHEN SCHOOLDAYS WERE FUN

A Lighthearted Look at "The Best Days of Our Lives"

STEPHEN BROWNING

HALSGROVE

370.962

First published in Great Britain in 2010

British Library Cataloguing-in-Publication Data
A CIP record for this title is available from the British Library

ISBN 978 0 85704 035 0

HALSGROVE
Halsgrove House,
Ryelands Industrial Estate,
Bagley Road, Wellington, Somerset TA21 9PZ
Tel: 01823 653777   Fax: 01823 216796
email: sales@halsgrove.com

Part of the Halsgrove group of companies
Information on all Halsgrove titles is available at: www.halsgrove.com

Printed and bound by SRP Ltd., Exeter

Contents

I dedicate this book to my brother, Nigel

How this Book Came About

This book came about during a meal in a Norwich pizza restaurant with my publisher, Simon Butler of Halsgrove.

We had been discussing another book at the time – *Norwich*, which has since been published and very well received, I am delighted to say: it was shortlisted for the EDP/East Anglian Awards 2009.

I was toying with a breadstick and wondering how a restaurant could charge £12.95 for an admittedly fresh piece of dough, coated in tomato purée and topped by some parmesan cheese and a few rocket leaves, when Simon said: 'We have been having great interest in our new series 'When things – Motoring and Holidays are two best-sellers – were Fun. A little retro – warm and funny, reminding people of times gone by, tho' not so long ago.'

I said, 'we could do 'When Life was Fun – mind you, it might end about 1700'.

'I was thinking about Schooldays', he laughed, calling for the bill. 'Could you do that?'

'Oh yes', I said. 'Oh, yes, indeed.'

Several weeks later, Simon came to my house and delivered about 100 books in the 'Halsgrove Community History' series: 'in case you need inspiration'. These wonderful books are accounts of life in all manner of small communities in the UK over the ages. Most of them have a chapter on 'Schooldays'. I spent many happy hours reading them. They form the backbone of this book, and the vast majority of the photographs come from them.

Thus inspired, I investigated local libraries, charity bookshops (lots there) and one-off contacts. I have had a great time. I have visited Shakespeare, Dickens, 'Tom Brown', 'Flashman' and writers, now long forgotten, who deserve a greater audience. I have discovered some lovely publications, some from long ago, on school histories, food, discipline, teachers, lessons and so on. And, of course, I have talked to many people who almost universally began by saying that they could not remember anything from their time at school but, with a little prompting, found that they could recall fascinating stories about teachers, dinners, rules or whatever. Their details are all included. So, thanks to everyone.

NOTE. Although the people mentioned in the book are real, I have, in all cases, changed their names. I have also changed the name of my Primary Boarding School.

Chapter One

Facing the School Day

And then the whining schoolboy, with his satchel,
And shining morning face, creeping like a snail
Unwillingly to school.
SHAKESPEARE *As You Like It*

Knowledge enormous makes a God of me.
JOHN KEATS

Getting There

The quote by Shakespeare is probably the most famous in the world about getting to school. Who does not have similar memories?

We have also all, I am sure, given unconvincing reasons for being late for school. Here is one, from the Halsgrove Community History Series, detailing a tale from the beginning of the last century that is so unlikely it could not have been made up:

Maybe you could get your little brother to lead you on a pony? This picture was taken at Hill farm, Brockamin, Worcestershire c.1945.

Waiting for the Twelfth Egg

Miss Lincoln used to teach the older children. Of course when I lived at the bottom of the lane I used to bring eggs to Mash's shop, a dozen, and take them back in grosses. Well that Miss Lincoln used to teach us. I'd got 11 eggs but I'd got to wait until the hen had laid the twelfth. Every time that character went up the yard and they'd have a look and say 'no he hasn't laid'. I said 'I can't wait much longer'. Well I went into school that day – they'd mark the register about quarter to ten – I should think it was a quarter past ten, and do you know that there Miss Lincoln couldn't cane me for laughing. She said 'why are you this late?' I said 'well I had to wait until the hen had done laying'. 'Well' she said 'How do you know the hen was going to lay laying?' I said 'Well it was sitting on the nest and I said my mother wanted to make it up to a dozen eggs 'cos I'd got to take the equivalent grosses back when I was coming home from school'. She was a'laughing so much she couldn't cane me.

The following is a description of getting to school in Norfolk a few decades later taken from *The Book of Blofield and Hemblington* by Barbara Pilch. It is perhaps surprising that the speaker, Charlie Howes, survived his childhood!

Eric Bates' journey to school from his home in Globe Lane was often exciting, Using his mother's bike, he would gather friends as he went along, ending up with six boys clinging on. He would pedal the bike while David Rope sat on his shoulders, John Ward might be on the carrier, and three boys from Shiels Court boys' home would take up positions on the pins at the front facing backwards, between the saddle and handlebars and making a second on the carrier. As they gathered speed down the hill they

You could always take the bus to school if your parents could afford it: this is the first bus in Mere, Wiltshire in 1913.

Or how about a donkey cart?

Maybe you could persuade the local farmer to take you on his cart? This photograph was taken in 1938.

Or how about riding in style on a magnificent Shire Horse – this photo was taken in 1944.

My earliest photo with my brother, Nigel, sitting in front: I seem to be saying 'Get off my pram!'

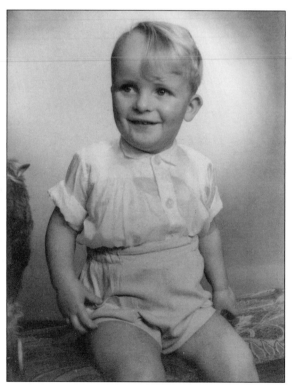

Me as a very young scallywag.

Looking overfed and dressed in a silk shirt, I seem to remember being terrified by the stuffed bird on the edge of the bed.

Getting the hang of this beach thing! At Weston-Super-Mare, where my dad ran a beach-front café: my fellow conspir-ators are my brother, Nigel and my sister, Juliet.

hoped that the gate into the playground would be left open!

For me, personally, getting to Primary school was a game of two halves, so to speak. I was fine, even cocky, if the homework the night before had been English or History, and I couldn't wait to show off in class. If, on the other hand, it had been something alien and incomprehensible like Maths or Physics, I would be on the edge of tearful funk until the inevitable, terrible humiliation came about. 'Stand up, Browning, and describe the essential qualities of an isosceles trian-gle'. What does a six year old boy want with an isosceles triangle? Oh Dear.

Most of my generation were bussed to school, unless, like the boy in Shakespeare's play, you were lucky enough to live close by. The bus, I remember, was a world unto itself where Primary school hierarchy was worked out: if you took lunch to school, you would soon know your place in the scheme of things by how much – if any – of your lunchbox remained by the time you got off at the school gates. Alternatively, it might be filled with ill-gotten gains – jam tarts, sherbet dabs, blackjacks and four-a-penny fruit salads.

Left: *My earliest fully conscious memory. I insisted on carrying this glass bottle along the seafront at Weston-Super-Mare, even though I was told to give it to my Nanny. Of course, I dropped it and it smashed but I recall Nanny being very kind and saying 'That's alright, sweetheart'.*

There was lots of fun to be had along the way. You might hit the back of the driver's head with a well-aimed conker; you could start up a smutty song or swap marbles: if you didn't have any good ones, it was fine to take Warner's, 'cos his father was a pacifist and rumoured to be – Oh God! – a vegetarian, so he didn't count. Pressing your face against the windows and making threatening gestures to the people on the pavement was fun - unless you were really stupid like Jessop who made an unforgiveable sign to a pedestrian just before the bus was due to pull up at the school gates. The angry man charged on to the bus, grasped the unfortunate boy by the collar – you could do that then – and marched him to the head where he got a good caning,

Left: *School holidays were spent in a caravan in the glorious woodlands of Surrey . What a wonderful yacht! I would sail it on the many lakes and rivers: once, it became becalmed in the middle of Frensham Waters and my Mum had to row out to retrieve it. I am aged about 6 here.*

the pain of which was nothing to the humiliation he suffered from his peers for several days . I remember a particular stop where some girls from another school waited for their bus. As we approached, several of the girls would undo a button on the top of their blouse and the bus would lurch alarmingly to the left as all the boys (except Warner, who considered it unseemly) would pile on to the seats on that side for a good view. The distraught driver would screech the bus to a halt and manhandle the boys back to their seats. If you wanted to kill a bit of time you could make out he had hurt you and that you were paralysed down your left side. Oh, what fun it all was!

When I was six and a half, I was enrolled in a private boarding school, Hickstons, in a Norfolk village. I remember Mum dropping me, my brother Nigel, two years my senior, and sister, Juliet, off after a long day's drive. Oh the tears! Eventually, Mum drove away and I rushed to my brother and grasped his hand. 'Get lost!', he said: thus I had my first lesson in how uncool it was to mix with a pupil in a year lower than yours, even if he was your brother.

As well as my initial arrival, I well remember my departure at the end of term one. When you are small, little things mean a lot. All of us boys vied with each other in crazy tales about how much money our parents earned, what big cars we had etc. At the end of my first term at Hickstons, my joy at seeing my Mum again was heightened immeasurably by the

I pose proudly in my first suit, aged about 7.

knowledge that she would come to pick me up in our brand new car – a Vauxhall estate in shades of pale and deep green (I had seen the picture). I was standing with my best friend Douglas outside the school, cases packed, when – Joy of Joys! – I saw this beautiful estate car coming up the drive.

'That's my Mum, come to get me in our new car!'

Suddenly, as my Mum swished round in the school drive, there was an awful clanking sound and lots of sparks. The exhaust had fallen off.

Douglas looked at me with a condescending smile. 'Yes, well, that's what happens when you can only afford a cheap car. Ah, here's my Dad in his Humber Super Snipe'.

Ghostly goings-on

The boarding house was about five miles from the school proper, which was a lovely rectory set in several acres of ground – built in early Victorian times when vicars lived and acted like the country gentry. This rectory held terrors of its own. Notably, on the second floor at the southern end of the main corridor, was a curious set of steps – about four, swing right, about three. There was a heavy wooden door and, inside, a small room with a ridiculously high ceiling with a stout beam across it. In the middle of the room was a blue and white ceramic toilet. It bore the legend 'Curio & Co, Watercloset Manufacturers 1834', and was decorated all over with blue flowers. Quite beautiful in its way. Anyway, none of us would go near it because schoolboy legend had it that a maid to the original vicar had got herself pregnant by the footman and, deserted, had hung herself from beam in the ceiling. Her ghost was to be seen, apparently, entering the toilet in tears, although exactly when I never did discover: many and many a time I hurried past that spot as a six and seven year old, heart pumping and eyes averted. Recently, researching this book, I went back to the rectory – it has been converted into spacious flats now – and was fortunate enough to meet one of the lady residents. 'Is my memory a childhood fantasy?' I asked. 'No, she is still around,' she replied. 'None of the residents have ever seen her, but some claim to have heard her weeping.'

We have a wee accident

Every morning, all the school – mainly primary boys but some secondary, too – would travel from the

Schoolchildren coming home from Rattery School, Devon, around 1900.

A picture of Mulbarton School, Norfolk, around 1902. Note that, although scrubbed up and dressed in their finest clothes, there is no disguising the mud on some children's boots as many would have walked a long way to school.

boarding house to the rectory in a blue double-decker bus, long past its prime, driven by the headmaster, Reverend Quantock. It was quite a nice ride, really, and a chance to see the unique lavender fields of the Norfolk countryside. I always travelled on the top deck. One day, for some reason, the road was blocked and the good Reverend decided to take 'the scenic route' via some country lanes. We had just entered a dark, tree-shrouded part of the road when, of a moment, the bus shuddered and, like the *Titanic*, began to lurch and keel over to the right. What had happened was that the two right-side wheels had left the tarmac just where the roadway was several feet above the surrounding scrubland. Over and over we went, very slowly, until there was a thwack, and I found myself lying on my side covered in shattered glass and seats, all of which appeared to have broken loose. The bus had come to rest on its side. A hand came through the wreckage towards me. 'Stephen, Stephen, are you OK?' It was my brother, Nigel.

'Yes, I think so'.

'Thank goodness. I don't want to have to tell Mummy you're dead'.

No-one was seriously hurt – the reason we had gone over 'in slow motion' was that the bus has come off the road at precisely the point where several heavy-duty telegraph poles lined the road and they had let us down slowly. I remember one snatch of conversation on the rescue bus which took us back to the boarding house – we had the day off school, hooray! I was sitting with my brother and the Reverend was seated in front. Nigel said: ' We are all safe, now'.

I said ' let's hope this one does not turn over!'

The Headmaster, Reverend Quantock, whipped round and thundered 'you are an utterly stupid little boy'.

A sack race is taking place on the lawn in from of the rectory at Mulbarton, Norfolk, early 1960s. These are exact contemporaries of the author and could well have been a photograph of his own school.

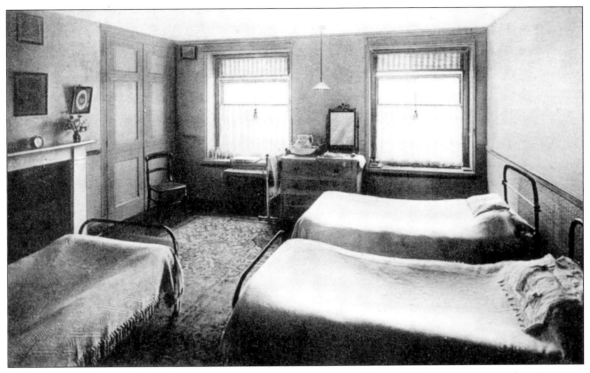

This picture of a dormitory in Western House School near Fareham, Hants, in 1925, reminds me precisely of my first school dormitory at Hickstons aged 6 and a half. We went to bed at seven o'clock unless, once in a while, we were invited to Matron's room to listen to the radio (BBC, naturally) for half an hour over a cup of cocoa – talk about happiness!

This picture of a class at St Decuman's Private Boys' School, Somerset, in the 1920s and administered by the Revd William Burgess (at back) has much of the Hickstons air about it.

Chapter Two

Schooldays – A Brief History

Nam et ipsa scientia potestas est
Knowledge itself is power.
FRANCIS BACON 1561 -1626

The battle of Waterloo was won on the playing fields of Eton.
THE DUKE OF WELLINGTON

It was not alway so...

It is easy for those of us alive now, and who received an education from the age of five or so, to assume that our ancestors fared likewise. Not so, at all. The most striking feature, of course, is that, until mid-Victorian times, any education on offer in the sense that we know it was just for men. The idea of educating a woman in, say, History, Physics, Maths or Philosophy never occurred to anyone, least of all the women themselves.

In medieval times, only boys – and just those, furthermore, at the top of society – were deemed worth the effort. If you wanted to be a diplomat, a statesman, an ambassador or a priest, then you might learn Latin – for this was the international language – along with etiquette, archery and how to drink your peers under the table: most of the public schools and universities established in the 13th and 14th centuries were entirely unsupervised after dinner and often struck terror into surrounding towns and villages.

Following the great victories at Crecy and Agincourt England began to get a fine idea of its own importance and also a feeling of security unknown before. Ideas became fashionable in top society, none more than the question of education – what is it for? Philosophy, reading, writing, arithmetic and religion became fashionable dinner and court topics. Some of the UK's most famous schools were founded at this time, including Winchester (1382), Eton (1440) and St Pauls (1518), the model being copied up and down the land.

Henry VIII went further. Largely using the money stripped from the suppression of the monasteries, he encouraged a new type of school – the 'grammar' model. These schools lowered the bar just a little so that you might get an education if you were a member of the landed gentry, the son of a distinguished officer in the army or navy, or even the son of a wealthy industrialist (tho' best not to mention it at school as being 'in trade' was – and still is, really – seen as very much second best). Medieval Latin was deemed 'corrupt' and replaced by classical Latin and Greek. Book learning became more common, thus lessening the soul-deadening practice of learning huge chunks of, often Latin, material by rote. Most revolutionary of all, a few eminent thinkers proposed that school should actually be a happy place – not a place of flogging – and that people from different backgrounds might mix together sometimes, on a very limited basis, naturally. Thus, the modern idea of 'schooldays' – having a rounded education, making friends from different classes, having some fun, and learning to think as well as being flogged , can legitimately be said to have begun at this time.

The pendulum swung back and forth after this period – for instance, following the restoration of Charles II, the encouragement of equality was seen as precisely the cause of the recent instability: grammar schools, in particular, were left to rot without state funding or support.

Don't Educate the Workers

All of this excitement over the years passed the workers by. With some periodic exceptions, the prevailing thought was that it was not a good idea to educate the workers because they might become

Infants School, Mill Lane, Carshalton, near Croydon, around 1870.

Left: *A class photograph of Haughley School, Suffolk, in the 1880s. As can be seen here, even the smallest boys wore hobnail boots.*

Sunday best, around 1908/9: this is the Trask children from the West Country village of West Coker.

The Gulliver children of Carhampton, Somerset, in their finest togs, about 1900.

The Methodist Chapel Sunday School, Northwood, Isle of Wight in 1895. Note the popularity of sailor suits for the boys, beautiful frocks for the girls and splendid hats for both.

Locks Green School infants class, Isle of Wight, around 1915.

discontented with 'going up one furrow and down another'. Trade training was OK - a very capable man might become apprenticed to a silversmith, farrier or signwriter, but these were all 'hands-on' things. Although some cities, Norwich in Norfolk being the first half way through the 17th century, established libraries of sorts, access to these was restricted to the upper classes – give the common man knowledge and who knows what might happen? By the middle of the 18th century, working class children had ceased to go to school at all. The French Revolution in 1789 triggered terror in the minds of government ministers, and any remaining educational scraps were quickly whipped away from the lower orders

Also, as the British Empire grew, cannon fodder was needed. By the time of the Battle of Waterloo in 1805 it was deemed unpatriotic to speak of letting working people escape the station into which God had wisely placed them – at the very bottom of the heap. On the battlefield, the English common man was a ferocious enemy – " I don't know what they do to the enemy', Wellington remarked, 'but, by God, they terrify me'.

Such 'Ladies Academies' as there were concentrated on preparing girls from rich backgrounds for a good marriage. These were especially popular in the 18th century and taught elegance, deportment, dancing, greetings, getting in and out of carriages, paying visits, along with a smattering of literary quotes from the favourite authors of the day to denote a cultured mind. At the end of the Victorian period, things changed with a vengeance – some academies taught practical subjects like cooking, sewing, house management and those at the real cutting edge, business practice. Many of the top girls' public schools date from this period.

Queen Victoria, a feisty young woman who knew her own mind, came to the throne in 1837. She showed concern for all her citizens from top to bottom. Society in general, and schooldays in particular, were about to undergo a revolution, but it would take until the beginning of the next century for the new liberal ideas to bear fruit. In many ways, modern society started here.

She was heavily influenced by the great love of her life, Prince Albert who, before his premature death, championed education and, importantly, the practical application of it to all aspects of life. The incomparable monument to him in Kensington Gardens denotes him sitting in majesty surrounded by – well,

actually sitting *on* – the greatest thinkers of civilisation from Ancient Greek times to the present.

Know your place

That the class basis of the education system existed thirty years after the Queen's accession is laid bare in the Taunton Commission Report of 1864, which looked at education for all classes 'between the humblest and the very highest.' Schooling was divided into three classes: the first grade was for what we should today call the upper middle class – sons of the professional classes, gentry and successful business people. These students could stay at school until they were 18 or 19 and prepare for university. The second grade would teach future shopkeepers, farmers and less eminent professional people. They would, however, be required to leave at 16 years so as to prevent them from going to university. All others lower down the social scale would form the third group for whom schooldays would cease at the age of 14.

The overriding idea was to keep people in their allotted place and, incredible as it seems today when the government has gone completely to the other extreme, to *prevent* all but a tiny elite from going on to higher education. The system, largely brought into place by an Act of 1869, also sought to stop anyone but the established upper classes from making money. If you were an enterprising chap with a good business brain, you could indeed become rich as many did – witness Samuel Bignold of Norwich Union and Jeremiah Colman, famous for his mustard – but you would receive absolutely no help from the education system in your quest. And once at the top of your profession, unless your family managed to marry into some cash-strapped branch of the established social order, which many did, you would find yourself branded as merely a 'higher tradesman' and top society would remain off-limits.

The Workhouse and Dame schools

So, if you were not one of the privileged, what educational options did you have? First off, if you were destitute, there was the poor house. Following the 1834 Poor Law Amendment Act, families were generally split up and children taken from parents; toys were confiscated. Any talking between parents and children was likely forbidden. Each person was forcibly washed and allocated a crude bed, most probably with at least one other stranger. In *The Book of Homersfield*, Ken Palmer gives an affecting descrip-

TABLE 1: DIETARY FOR AGED AND INFIRM PAUPERS

		Breakfast Bread	Cooked Meat	Dinner Potatoes	Soup	Sweet or Rice Pudding	Supper Bread	Cheese
		oz.	oz.	oz.	pt	oz.	oz.	oz.
SUN	Men	6	4	24		5		
	Women	5	4	24		4		
MON	Men	6		6	1½		5	1½
	Women	5		6	1½		4	1½
TUES	Men	6	4	24			5	
	Women	5	4	24			4	
WED	Men	6		6	1½		5	1½
	Women	5		6	1½		4	1½
THUR	Men	6	4	24			5	
	Women	5	4	24			4	
FRI	Men	6		12	1½	10	5	1½
	Women	5		12	1½	8	4	1½
SAT	Men	6		6	1½		5	1½
	Women	5		6	1½		4	1½

People of 60 years of age to be allowed 1 oz. tea, 4 oz. butter, 5 oz. sugar per week. The sick to be dieted as directed by Medical Officers.

TABLE 2: DIETARY FOR ABLE-BODIED MEN AND WOMEN

		Breakfast Bread	Gruel	Cooked Meat	Dinner Potatoes	Soup	Sweet or Rice Pudding	Supper Bread	Cheese	Broth
		oz.	pt	oz.	oz.	pt	oz.	oz.	oz.	pt
SUN	Men	6	1½	4	24			6		1½
	Women	5	1½	4	24			5		1½
MON	Men	6	1½		6	1½		6	2	
	Women	5	1½		6	1½		5	2	
TUES	Men	6	1½	4	24			6		1½
	Women	5	1½	4	24			5		1½
WED	Men	6	1½		6	1½		6	2	
	Women	5	1½		6	1½		5	2	
THUR	Men	6	1½	4	24			6		1½
	Women	5	1½	4	24			5		1½
FRI	Men	6	1½		16		10	6	2	
	Women	5	1½		16		8	5	2	
SAT	Men	6	1½		6	1½		6	2	
	Women	5	1½		6	1½		5	2	

Basic rations at the Union Workhouse, Cerne Abbas, seven miles north of Dorchester in Dorset.

tion of what happened next. Women and girls commonly sat spinning hemp or carding wool. Men and boys worked in the fields for local farmers or repaired roads, collecting and breaking stones. The Shipmeadow House of Industry, which he highlights in the book and which opened in 1767, saved money by apprenticing children to local tradesmen. Sometimes, as everyone knows from Dickens' *Oliver Twist*, boys were 'sold', perhaps to a chimney sweep or maybe a window cleaner and, in Oliver's case, to a coffin maker. Oliver had a particularly sad countenance and a was a perfect and highly lucrative choice to precede the funeral procession – , and this at a time when grime had to be literally scraped off most city windows. Punishment for naughty boys and girls at Shipmeadow – the most common wrongdoing was leaving the house without permission from the governor – entailed going without meat during the following week and repeating the offence would result in a yellow jacket being worn at mealtimes. Those mealtimes consisted of a daily diet of gruel, bread and cheese with soup, bacon and potatoes or meat and potatoes once a week.

Not every Victorian thought workhouses were a good idea. One of my favourite poems is by that 19th century *bon viveur* and breeder of bulldogs, George R. Sims. Although largely forgotten today, he became very rich and famous in his time, producing a string of poems and best-selling novels.

Mercy Swain, matron and wife of the Union Workhouse master, Alfred Swain, with the workhouse children, 1890s, in Bakewell of pudding fame. Note that girls and boys are dressed in the same manner.

Christmas Day in the Workhouse
by George R. Sims

It was Christmas Day in the Workhouse,
And the cold bare walls are bright
With garlands of green and holly,
And the place is a pleasant sight:
For with clean-washed hands and faces,
In a long and hungry line
The paupers sit at the tables,
For this is the hour they dine.

And the guardians and their ladies,
Although the wind is east,
Have come in their furs and wrappers,
To watch their charges feast;
To smile and be condescending,
Put pudding on pauper plates,
To be hosts at the workhouse banquet
They've paid for — with the rates.

Oh, the paupers are meek and lowly
With their 'Thank-ee kindly, mums',
So long as they fill their stomachs,
What matter it whence it comes?
But one of the old men mutters,
And pushes his plate aside:
'Great God', he cries: but it chokes me!
For this is the day she died'.

The guardians gazed in horror,
The master's face went white;
'Did a pauper refuse their pudding?'
'Could their ears believe aright?'
Then the ladies clutched their husbands,
Thinking the man would die,
Struck by a bolt or something,
By the outraged One on high.

The poem is a long one and goes on to record how, the previous Christmas, his wife had been refused food by the workhouse and died as a result. It ends:

'Yes, there in a land of plenty,
Lay a loving woman dead,
Cruelly starved and murdered
For a loaf of parish bread.
At yonder gate, last Christmas,
I craved for a human life.
You, who would feast us paupers,
What of my murdered wife!

'There, get ye gone to your dinners;
Don't mind me in the least;
Think of the happy paupers
Eating your Christmas feast;
And when you recount their blessings
In your smug parochial way,
Say what you did for me, too,
Only last Christmas Day'.

A schoolroom, early 1900s: this one is quite cosy with an open fire.

Workhouses continued until 31 March 1930: many people alive today have parents whose only education, if it can be so-laughingly called, came from these places.

Then there were the Dame schools. If you could find such a school, and there were some, run by a gentlewoman of reduced means, you were extremely fortunate. Mostly these entirely unregulated houses of terror were set up by anyone at all – not always a dame; maybe a soldier who had lost a leg at Waterloo, a defrocked parson, or a drunk. We even have an account of a Dame school where the elderly woman presiding over it was so ill she could not get out of bed.

If you had a little money, or even, like Mr Dombey, a great deal but were mean with it, there were a huge variety of schools, mostly of the boarding type, that would take your child for a fee. These could be good, bad or terrible, mostly the last. In 1848, Charles Dickens highlighted Mrs Pipchin to whose establishment in Brighton, young Paul Dombey was sent:

The celebrated Mrs Pipchin was a marvellous ill-favoured, ill-conditioned old lady, of a stooping figure, with a mottled face like bad marble, a hook nose, and a hard grey eye, that looked as if it might have been hammered at on an anvil without sustaining any injury. Forty years at least had elapsed since the Peruvian mines had been the death of Mr Pipchin; but his relict still wore black bombazeen, of such a lustreless, deep, dead, sombre shade, that gas itself couldn't light her up after dark, and her presence was a quencher to any number of candles. She was generally spoken of as a 'great manager' of children; and the secret of her management was, to give them everything that they didn't like, and nothing that they did – which was found to sweeten their dispositions very much. She was such a bitter old lady, that one was tempted to believe there had been some mistake in the application of the Peruvian machinery, and that all her waters of gladness and milk of human kindness had been pumped out dry, instead of the mines.

Her modern equivalent would be the Death Eaters from the Harry Potter books – these suck out your breath and, with it, all joy. I have often thought that

The workhouse wash-house in Bitterne, a suburb of Southampton, about 1905.

Dickens would greatly admire, even perhaps envy a little, J.K. Rowling's creations. Although separated by a hundred and something years, both authors tell tales about love, friendship, loyalty and youthful struggle: both also achieved world-wide success on an astonishing scale.

Dr Blimber's establishment, to which young Paul was also sent, was not malign, just cold and incompetent:

Doctor Blimber's establishment was a great hot-house, in which there was a forcing apparatus incessantly at work. All the boys blew before their time. Mental green-peas were produced at Christmas and intellectual asparagus all the year round. Mathematical gooseberries (very sour ones, too) were common at untimely seasons, and from mere sprouts of bushes, under Dr Blimber's cultivation. Every description of Greek and Latin vegetable was got off the driest twigs of boys, under the frostiest circumstances. Nature was of no consequence at all. No matter what a young gentleman was intended to bear, Dr Blimber made him bear to pattern, somehow or other.

Dickens was at his best when in a rage, which, as far as education and the treatment of young people was concerned, was most of the time.

Inspectors come calling

Slowly, as the government enlarged the work of Inspectors, Dame schools and the worst independent schools, were phased out. *The Book of Sennen* by Sennen Local History Group gives an account of an inspection of the Dame school in Skewjack, at the most westerly tip of Cornwall, in 1852: 'The buildings are very bad; floor full of holes, windows broken, very exposed, nor any care devolving on any person'. The furniture was poor and the children played either in the road in front of the school or on the common. There was a poor supply of books, no apparatus, and learning was confined to reading from tattered bibles and a few testaments, spelling a few words and writing in copybooks. At other Dame schools, any learning can perhaps be charitably termed 'erratic'. It consisted of whatever the dame could teach – maybe sewing, butter-making, learning the Lord's Prayer and other religious tracts or learning to count a little.

Inspectors had a beneficial effect on schools for most. One million pupils were inspected in 1870. For the first time, in 1900, Board schools came to outnumber religious and all other types of schools. Specially trained officers were charged with getting children to school. Mayhew's writings on the condition of the poor of London caused outrage and shock when they were first published in the mid 1800s, depicting an underclass of children, verminous and lice-ridden, who existed in deserted cellars and under the smoke-filled arches of the city.

Later, the Boer War exposed the extent of malnutrition and lack of education in new recruits. As a new King, Edward VII, came to the throne in 1901, the nation demanded a new dawn as far as young people and their schooling was concerned.

Snow storms, sore feet and very basic sanitation

There were now officers empowered to make sure children went to school. Parents of the poor were unimpressed, even hostile. Children, as will be discussed later, had something better to do than go to school – work. Stephanie Pouya, in *The Book of Sampford Courtenay with Honeychurch* depicts an exasperated William Manuell, appointed Headmaster of the local school at the young age of 21 struggling to keep his school open in the face of attendance which was, successively 'wretchedly', 'shockingly', 'dreadfully', 'miserably' and 'frightfully' bad.

The much-feared school attendance officer! This is Mr William Lightfoot Hague with his family. Mr Hague lived in Blofield, just outside Norwich.

In rural areas, just getting to school was a major enterprise. In *The Book of Sennen*, Jane Hicks remembers how, at the beginning of the new century, she would walk a mile and a half across the fields to school taking her lunch of 'figgy-oggen' – a small pasty filled with raisins – with her; maybe other days she would have an egg pasty or gingerbread sandwiches, which had home-made biscuit as a filling. The records kept by William Manuell a few years earlier give us a glimpse into what could go wrong:

14.11.1887   Several children absent with sore feet.
8.12.1887   Attendance today very bad owing to rain.
10.3.91   Snow storms still raging. Impossible for children to attend school. Closed school for the week.

At school, conditions were hardly conducive to learning. Often schools relied on parents contributing a fixed amount per week to keep the school running, a practice that was not at all popular and so money was tight. Rural schools were often heated by

An oven-in-the-wall in Hemblington school, Norfolk: these were sucessors to the 'tortoise' stoves which gave off large amounts of smoke but very little heat.

'tortoise' stoves: the children would lay their wet clothes on them to dry. In any event, they produced little warmth as this 1911 government report into Sampford Courtenay school shows: ' Both rooms are terribly cold and the children certainly suffered and could not possibly have done any work to best advantage… Snow is actually falling in the infants' room this morning'.

Lavatories were basic. Here is a pupil's recollections of a rural school's arrangements in the 1920s:

Neither electricity nor water supply was ever connected to the school. Oil lamps were used for lighting and bucket lavatories and portable washbasins were across the yard. Water had to be brought each day by the caretaker, Becky Horn, collected from the standpipe near the carpenter's shop. Becky, helped by her husband, George, had the job of emptying the lavatory buckets into a large pit in the school grounds. There were doors at the back of the lavatories to extract the contents. According to Len Piper, some naughty boys would poke stinging nettles through the gaps. There was one heck of a do once because it was a teacher in there!

After 1918, after the sacrifices made by the working classes in the War, education and elementary education entered the modern age – ie, it was seen as a right. Elementary education was completely free for the first time and government help was increased for secondary schools. Those that were built from this time boasted playing fields and even swimming pools.

If the medieval period can be described as 'Schooldays for some of the people some of the time' and the Victorian and Edwardian eras as 'Schooldays for most of the people most of the time', the period following the First World War until the 1980s can be seen as 'Schooldays for all'.

A wonderfully energetic picture of the pupils of the village school, Nynehead, seven miles from Taunton in Somerset, taken in 1988.

The children were much more sedate in this picture, taken in 1908!

My, this looks cold!

An unusual school day! This tree had crashed in the garden of Mr Leggett, landlord of the Kings Head in Hempnall, south of Norwich, and the following day these schoolchildren posed for a picture. The date is July 1907.

In the early twentieth century, a combination of new ideas about the curriculum and a concern for the health of the nation's young produced new and radical ideas about subjects that should be taught in schools. Here, in Hampshire, are boys of Bitterne School's gardening class posing for the camera with squeaky-clean gardening implements and dressed in their best Sunday clothes.

A day of peace celebrations for the schoolchildren of Seaton, Devon, in 1919.

Chapter Three
We Are All Good at Something

Multiplication is vexation,
Division is as bad,
The Rule of three doth puzzle me,
And Practice drives me mad.
ELIZABETHAN POEM 1570

We would all be idle if we could.
SAMUEL JOHNSON 1776

The poor man!

The most unpopular subject in my secondary school was the oldest in the curriculum – religious studies.

We were a class of 15 year olds – top stream in the grammar so we were pretty cocky and obnoxious. In previous years we had been taught religion by any teacher who happened to have a free lesson. Now, for the first time, the school had managed to appoint a specialist – a slight man with black trousers and an overlarge white shirt.

At teacher training college they will tell you, when first meeting a new class, to 'get their interest'. I well remember from my own teaching days that all can be won or lost in the first ten minutes. A gentle year or three terms of purgatory may hinge on these initial moments. Students smell fear and feast on flaws, but if you get their interest and respect they will prove the staunchest of allies, not least when the dreaded Inspector comes along and asks 'is it OK if I just sit in on your class?'

It was lesson number one. New Mr Mottle – for such was his name – went in guns blazing.

'Good morning boys, we are going to talk about sex. In particular, we are going to consider members.'.

'Members of what, Sir?'

'Male members – what is your name – Rudge – yes, yours included and how it relates to ethics. Ethics in turn relate to one's religious beliefs.'

'Oh, that sounds very interesting, Sir. I have a query, Sir?'

'Yes, Jessop, what is it?'

'I was reading the parliamentary debates in *The Times*, Sir, and it said that members should always be erect and upstanding. Would you agree with that, Sir?'

'And, Sir,' broke in Yardot, a frail youth in the fourth row, 'the Foreign Secretary is going to resign. Someone in the House of Commons said that it would always be proud of its illustrious member. Was he talking about politics or sex or ethics, Sir? It is very confusing?'

'Please explain to us, Sir'. Sage nods up and down the classroom.

'Oh Dear, my poor Dad'. It was Jessop again.

'Is your father ill, Jessop?'

'I think he must be, Sir. Last night, he came home from his gardening club and said they had a problem with declining members.'

'That is enough, boys' rallied Mr Mottle. He put a chalk mark on the blackboard. 'What is that?'

'It is a chalk mark on the blackboard, Mr Tottle'. Murmers of concurrence amongst the assorted members.

'Mottle', Jones. 'I know you don't know me very well, yet, but the name is Mr Mottle'.

'Sorry, Sir'

'Now one thing about the male member is that it is an imprecise instrument'.

'Is it an instrument, Mr Pottle? Good Grief!'

'Mottle. Mottle. Now, you could not aim it at this spot on the blackboard as it is, well, imprecise, and this is interesting in relation to sexual ethics.'

The class was stunned into silence. Surely there had never been a lesson with such potential for wisdom.

At last, White senior raised his hand. 'I have a question, Sir?'

'Yes, White, what is it?' Mr Mottle looked pleased – perhaps all would be well after all.

'It's about that white spot on the blackboard, Sir – aiming at it and so on. Well, Sir, unless you have got an exceptionally large one, isn't it a bit high, anyway?'

Mr Mottle lasted just the one term. A few weeks after our memorable class, I remember seeing him and his wife and two small children walking along the road a few hundred yards from the school. To my, no doubt jaundiced eye, he looked a little bent in his back and not very happy. I think he was a good man, but boys can be very cruel.

Religion was the very first and most important subject to be taught in schools: the Gods predominated in Greek and Roman society and the rulers and ruled had at least a moral compass – from which to deviate, perhaps, but it was still there. The Dark Ages were, well, *dark*, as society fell into a chasm of barbarism, confusion and sorcery. As schooling began again in the early Middle Ages, it was the clerics who drove it onward. And it was in the 15th century that leading citizens began to question whether the array of subjects taught should be widened.

What shall we teach them?

We now refer to the subjects taught in schools as the curriculum. 'Curriculum' derives from the Latin word 'racecourse' and thus a 'school curriculum' means the experiences a child will have to undergo and the hurdles he or she will need to overcome in order to emerge as a happy and well-rounded adult. Later, when applying for a job, we have to complete a 'Curriculum Vitae' which means, literally, 'Racecourse of Life' which seems pretty apt to me.

Incredibly, for a country which had built an Empire on which 'the sun never set', the first textbook on the

Aren't we smart? Children at Rattery School in Devon dress up for the camera, about 1908.

This is my Grandma with my Mum on her lap and my over-dressed Uncle Eric.

A most elegantly dressed young brother and sister, around 1902/3 – Albert 'Harry' Key and Kathleen from St Ervan, Cornwall.

A similar picture taken in 1923 of Eileen and Donald Pollard from Cornwall: the boys' stiff starched collars of the Victorian age have given way to softer, more elaborate styles.

Cornish lad, Garfield Lobb, models a much more modern looking best suit in 1928 as he stands proudly by his fabulous Meccano model.

Agnes Carpenter, Oliver and Reg pose in their very best, around 1916.

A much more simple style came into being in the 1940s as can be witnessed from these two evacuees to Crudwell in Wiltshire: they are brother and sister, Mary and Eddie Jones.

curriculum – what young people should learn in order to become good citizens and fulfilled individuals – was only published in 1918, when we were about to lose it. This last statement may be controversial as the Empire was not finally to unravel until after the Second World War but the fact that it did so at a breathtaking pace was largely because the signs of loss of power – in terms of trade to Russia, armaments to Germany and influence to America – were plainly visible as early as 1901. After the austerity of Queen Victoria's rule, however, everyone wanted a party and Edward VII was more than happy to lead it. None are so blind as those who will not see.

The Curriculum by John Franklin Bobbitt (1918) is a fine book, bearing in mind nothing like it had been written before and especially as he recognized that you can only do so much – albeit a lot – within school: he believed that young people also need to be educated in the family and in society as a whole. Both he and John Dewey, who wrote later, saw the curriculum as very much a way to mould a young person into an *ideal*. Nowadays, such a grand vision is decried, a curriculum being just the subjects you teach, the way they are taught and the methods used to assess them. No two schools or decades are quite the same, but from 1918 to the 1980s, a core curriculum would probably consist of the following subjects:

> Mathematics
> English Language
> English Literature
> Overseas Language – French, or German being
>   popular
> Latin (in grammar schools)
> History – probably British
> Geography
> Physics
> Chemistry
> Biology
> Art
> Religious education
> Liberal/General Studies
> Games – Football, Cricket, Hockey, Rugby,
>   Hockey, Tennis and Athletics

As mentioned in the last chapter, the more affluent members of society have always had an education of sorts available to them. Until relatively recently, however, members of the lower orders received very short shrift. Furthermore, whilst the affluent went from what we can roughly call 'Primary' to 'Secondary' school and hence to a university if they

wished, any 'schoolday scraps' thrown to the poor ended at age 10 or 11. So, until little more than 100 years ago, such history as there is concerning working class schooldays relates only to 'Primary' years.

You'll only make them discontented

Let us go back to 1780. The government was in more than two minds about education for the lower orders. They surely had a commitment to teach people to read, didn't they? Did that include writing, too? What about the bible – that could be a bit revolutionary with all that talk about equality and sharing food with your neighbours, couldn't it? If someone was content eating meat once a week, should they know about fine dining? Once farm labourers knew about the great finance houses of the City of London, surely they would want to sit in comfortable offices all day, adding up figures and drinking coffee? Show them the paintings of Michaelangelo and the works of Chaucer and they would surely give up work altogether?

Just across the Channel, France was in turmoil for precisely these reasons – the working classes had taken enough punishment: soon the Bastille would fall, aristocrats would end their lives on the guillotine and everyone in England, very much including the poor to whom Charles Dickens was a hero, would become familiar with *A Tale of Two Cities*.

The government's response was predictable: education must be discouraged for the common man. As has often happened in the history of these islands, however, as you push down the daisies in one part of the garden, up they will pop, in slightly different form, in another part. Thus we find men like Samuel Bamford and the self-educated Robert Owen setting up mutual improvement societies and reading circles. Most famous, perhaps, were the Mendip Schools, run by Hannah and Martha Moore and exuberantly supported by evangelical churches. These meetings, in towns and country areas throughout the land, were packed with keen youngsters. They had two features that we would find astonishing – they taught reading only, NOT writing, and they taught only those things useful to life as servants.

Behind this thinking is a perverse notion of Christianity that says in one and the same breath 'study the scriptures but do not try to improve your lot in life'. It is immortalized in literature by the plight of young Oliver Twist, starving and weak, drinking his daily gruel in the workhouse: on the wall in large letters is written 'God is Good'.

The workers start to read

It is hard to over-emphasize the liberation that reading gave people. Even if you could not read, you could pay someone to do it for you. And the poor man had a new emerging and influential champion in Charles Dickens. No writer had before empathized with the poor, their aspirations and sufferings to such a degree. Once catapulted to international fame at the age of 25 with *The Pickwick Papers*, Dickens published his great novels in monthly instalments. Some of his finest writing features the poor and their education, or lack of it. *Nicholas Nickleby*, in which schoolboys were sent to linger and die of neglect and malnutrition at Dotheboys Hall under the evil Mr Squeers and his tragi-comic family, is credited with being responsible for the abolition of such establishments. In *Hard Times*, he exposed the sterility of denying young people emotional and spiritual sustenance in favour of Mr Gradgrind's regime of 'facts, facts, facts!'

Great excitement was generated by the upcoming publication of each of Dickens' chapters, although he sometimes had trouble keeping up with demand. He himself recalls being in a local Rochester shop when a lady customer asks the shopkeeper whether he has the latest chapter of Mr Dickens' new novel. The shopkeeper replied ' No, Ma'am – it is due here in about ten days'. Dickens apparently thought to himself, in that case, that he must go home and start it! In another, maybe apocryphal, story a felon sentenced to the gallows in a month's time remarked to the judge 'Thank you, my Lord, I will at least be able to have the new chapter of *David Copperfield* read to me before I meet my maker.'

As mentioned, almost anyone could set up a school. Sometimes, as in the following advertisement in the *Salisbury and Winchester Journal* of 1842, and quoted in *The Book of Mere* by Dr David Longbourne, it was difficult to work out exactly what was to be taught:

Mere School, Conducted by Mr J A Lander, terms for Board and Instruction, Books, Perusal of Books in School Library and washing, £22 per annum. The above terms include every scholastic item. The experience Mr Lander has acquired during the long period he was engaged as resident master in Collegiate, metropolitan and other first-rate and extensive Establishments together with his adop-

tion of the most approved and modern methods which he has successfully applied in the mathematical preparation of gentlemen for the universities, Naval and Military Colleges, etc, tends in no small degree to expedite the improvement of pupils committed to his charge. No limitation of diet. Surveying will be practically taught in the field. A Christmas Examination Paper will be forwarded to any Parent on application.

Should everyone go to school?

Dickens died in 1870. Three years earlier virtually all men had been given the vote and there was much talk of compulsory education for all. Only a third of working class children attended any kind of school. The Foster Act of 1870 brought in a dual system of schools for primary pupils – state schools would co-exist with private and charitable ones. In *The Book of Sennen* we are reminded that the new system was very far from ideal:

'…the new schools would be maintained by boards elected from local people with the power to levy a rate – 3d in the pound – to be spent on education. Schooling wasn't compulsory and, since it cost parents as much as 9d a week in some places, when the average weekly wage of a farm labourer was about 11s, it often was not a realistic option. The poverty of Sennen Covers, who mostly relied on fishing for a living, at that time was desperate.'

The newly-built school and school house in Sennen in 1880 cost £1,300,172.10d which was £100 more than estimated. Much rancour resulted. The school was extended in 1894 to provide an infants' classroom which featured a Cornish range and 'slab' for heating and a well for water.

Pay for the staff was not good, records show. The master's annual salary in the 1890s was about £80 – not too bad, really, for the time. However, an assistant mistress received only about £35; a pupil teacher – a 'bright' student of anything from 12 to 18 years who taught pupils alongside getting on with his (always invariably at this time they were boys) own studies – about £12 and a monitoress about £5, slightly less than the caretaker.

Other such studies in the Community History Series show that how much parents paid varied greatly around the country – often this contribution, which was put alongside government grants, was called 'children's pence'. For example, in 1877, the weekly rates in Sampford Courtenay and Honeychurch were

Some immaculately dressed musicians with Mrs Gibson at Crudwell, Wiltshire, around 1900.

related to how much a person earned – farmers paid 6d each child, tradesmen and artisans 2d, labourers 1d. Infants were 1d for everyone and there was a special deal for parents enrolling more than two children – for all the above, half price for the third child and any thereafter.

Many parents could not see the point of educating the 'inside' of a child whilst 'doing nothing for the outside', and a form of protest was to send the boy or girl to school nearly naked: the clear challenge was 'do something about that, then'. Theoretically Board inspectors could enforce schooling until the age of ten, but such rules were generally treated with contempt as parents kept children at home, especially during the harvest season.

Brain fever and exhaustion

Worse was to come as far as parents were concerned. Until 1875 rote learning was the accepted method of teaching and English, writing and arithmetic were the standard subjects. From that year, however, grammar, geography, history and needlework were added: then, in 1890, cookery, wood and metal craft with some PE. Add to this local specialities, such as the teaching of Honiton Lace which was introduced in that town in 1908,' the teachers being Mrs Pease and Miss Trissie Knight, daughter of Samuel Knight, the bootmaker', and you have a very busy school

indeed. The ideas of Froebel – less cramming and more play, personal thought and happiness – became fashionable. How could the young ones cope? Parents worried that children would develop 'brain fever' and end up in mental hospitals.

From this time (very) limited voluntary school meals were available in some parts of the country. A top medical journal reported that children were becoming healthier and happier.

The strain on school teachers, coping with all this change, must have been great. William Manuell, the talented teacher who became a Headmaster in Devon at 21, died in 1893 aged only 38. He had not shown signs of illness: maybe he was just worn out. Richard Pyke, one of his students, wrote this of him:

'He died while still young, and many of the boys and girls shed tears as they sang 'Jesu, lover of my soul' by the graveside. He was a strict disciplinarian, a rather bigoted churchman with little sympathy for dissenters: but he was never unjust... I think his teaching must have been excellent: at any rate I was grounded well enough in the subjects taught to pursue my studies alone, without any confusion of mind.'

Parents, too, were reading more. The influence of Dickens has already been mentioned: add to this popular journals such as William Cobbett's *Twopenny*

My Grandad and Grandma on my Mother's side, about 1910. Although from working stock, they felt at ease posing for the camera in beautiful clothes and, significantly, both with an arm resting on a book to signify learning: it was about this time that improving one's station in life through education began to become a reality for some.

A very exciting learning experience – children with the bells ready to be rehung in St Michael's Church, Mere, Wiltshire, 1911.

Trash (1816), *Poor Man's Guardian* (1832), *Titbits* (1881), *Daily Mail* (1896), and the *Daily Mirror* (1904) and we are witnessing almost a whole population becoming literate in the space of a relatively few years.

Ah, the great Empire!

There was a sense of celebration in the air during the Edwardian period – from Edward VII's accession in 1901 to the start of the Great War in 1914. As remarked previously, the foundations of wealth and Empire may not have been as robust as they seemed, but on the surface there was glitter, elegance and a pervasive sense of national pride. The League of the Empire had been founded with Royal Patronage in 1896. Its mission was to bind the Empire together in perpetuity, principally by exchanging educational ideas and teachers. The first UK teachers went out to Canada and Australia in order to show how school-days were in England, the hub of the then known universe. Schools, many prospering today, were set up on the English model. Huge educational confer-ences, such as the 1919 Paris Conference, were set up attended by teachers from different lands. Soon, teachers had the idea of exchanging with each other and they, in turn brought their pupils. The League of the Empire, in a slimmed down form, still exists today, concentrating on exchanging teachers and headteachers between the UK and the 50 plus nations of the Commonwealth.

Empire Day, started by Lord Meath, was perhaps the biggest celebration in the school year: schools from Epsom to Madras and from Wellington to Alice Springs would spend a day festooned in red, white and blue bunting whilst listening to rousing speeches. We have the following intriguing sentence from the school report at Honiton :

'24.5.1922: It is Empire Day and the children have had a short address on their responsibilities and privileges as members of the British Empire'

One wonders what they were.

The national anthem would be played and all across the world people would have tea and settle down to a game of cricket. I have been privileged to research many of the original journals and reports of the League of the Empire during the years 1896 to 1920 and it is amazing how attitudes have shifted – there was not a shred of doubt at that time that the Empire was a wholly beneficial phenomenon, nor that it would not last for ever.

Bakewell Church Lads' Brigade, Derbyshire, symbolising the might of Empire around 1902.

HYMNS TO BE SUNG

AT THE

WESLEYAN SUNDAY SCHOOL TEA TREAT, MYLOR BRIDGE,

JULY 28*th*, 1869.

1st. PRAISE OF JESUS.

1. To thee, O blessed Saviour,
   Our grateful songs we raise ;
   Oh, tune our hearts and voices
   Thy holy name to praise.
   'Tis by thy sov'reign mercy
   We're here allowed to meet,
   To join with friends and teachers
   Thy blessing to entreat.

2. Oh, may thy precious gospel
   Be publish'd all abroad,
   Till the benighted heathen
   Shall know and serve the Lord,
   Till o'er the wide creation
   The rays of truth shall shine,
   And nations now in darkness
   Arise to light divine.

2nd. THE KING OF KINGS.

1. Low the infant Saviour lies,
   He appears in lowly guise ;
   Yet by faith we read the words—
   King of Kings and Lord of lords.

2. See ! he stands at Pilate's bar
   Most despised of all by far
   Still to him belong the words—
   King of Kings and Lord of lords.

3. He who wears the crown of thorns,
   He whom man reviles and scorns,
   Yet demands as his the words—
   King of kings and Lord of lords.

4. On the cross 'tis still the same ;
   Never can he yield his claim
   To those ever glorious words—
   King of kings and Lord of lords.

3rd. REST IN' CHRIST.

1. Awake my soul, in joyful lays
   To sing thy great Redeemer's praise,
   He justly claims a song from me ;
   His loving-kindness. O how free !

2. He saw me ruined by the fall,
   Yet loved me notwithstanding all
   He saved me from my lost estate
   His loving-kindness, O how great.

3. Often I feel my sinful heart
   Prone from my Saviour to depart ;
   But though I have him oft forgot
   His loving-kindness changes not.

4. Soon shall I pass the gloomy vale
   Soon all my mortal powers must fail.
   O may my last expiring breath
   His loving-kindness sing in death.

4th. THE GATHERING.

1. We gather, we gather, dear Jesus to bring
   The breathings of love, 'mid the blossoms of spring ;
   Our Maker ! Redeemer ! we gratefully raise
   Our hearts and our voices in hymning thy praise.
   Chorus—
   Hallelujah ! Hallelujah ! Hosannah in the highest.
   Hallelujah ! Hallelujah ! Hosannah to the Lord.

2. When stooping to earth from the brightness of heaven
   Thy blood for our ransom so freely was given !
   Thou deignest to listen while children adored,
   With joyful hosannas the blest of the Lord.
   Hallelujah, etc.

3. Those arms which embraced little children of old
   Still love to encircle the lambs of the fold ;
   That grace which invited the wandering home
   Hath never forbidden the youngest to come.
   Hallelujah, etc.

4. Hosannah ! hosannah ! Great Teacher we raise
   Our hearts and our voices in hymning thy praise
   For precept and promise so graciously given
   For blessings of earth and the glories of heaven
   Hallelujah, etc.

5th. HE WIPES THE TEAR.

1. When sore afflictions crush the soul,
   And riven is every earthly tie,
   The heart must cling to God alone—
   He wipes the tear from every eye.
   Thro' wakeful nights, when rack'd with pain,
   On bed of languishing you lie,
   Remember still that God is near ;
   He wipes the tears from every eye.

2. A few short years and all is o'er,
   Your sorrows—pain—will soon pass by :
   Then lean in faith on God's dear Son ;
   He wipes the tear from every eye.
   Oh, never be your soul cast down,
   Nor let your soul desponding sigh ;
   Assured that God, whose name is love,
   Will wipe the tear from every eye.

Gill & Son, Machine Printers, Penryn.

Hymn sheet for the Weslyan Sunday school tea treat, Mylor Bridge, Cornwall 1869. This is a good example of how evangelical Christianity was linked to the glory of Empire at this time:

Oh, may thy precious gospel
Be publish'd all abroad,
Till the benighted heathen
Shall know and serve the Lord,
Till o'er the wide creation
The rays of truth shall shine,
And nations now in darkness
Arise to light divine.

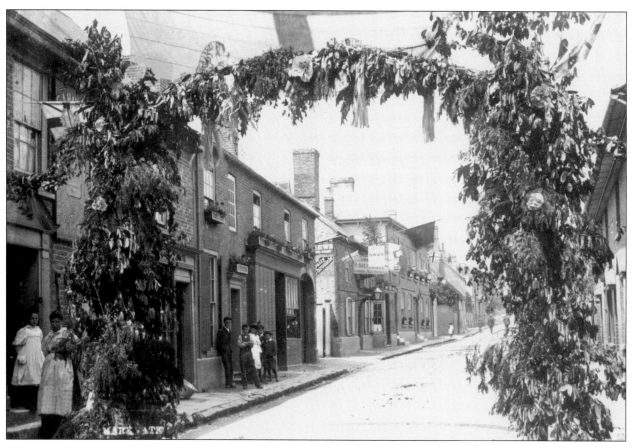

Many people may not have had much money but they were mighty proud of the Queen and Empire: here we see children and adults dressed in their Sunday best preparing to celebrate Queen Victoria's Diamond Jubilee in 1897 along the High Street in Markyate, Chiltern Hills.

All of which goes to explain the seemingly paradoxical attitude of the poorest of parents and their siblings at school – they may not have been getting much of the cake but they were mighty proud of the Empire. Following the 'War to end Wars', the government did, for the first time, decide that the families of the heroic soldiers should be given a lift by the state – elementary education was to be henceforth free for all. Also, female headteachers were allowed from 1921 and this freed up a greatly talented resource to help at school.

Right: *The height of schoolgirl fashion – Dora and Ivy Haydon of Carhampton, Somerset, about 1916.*

Mulbarton ladies hockey team, Norfolk, around 1907: it is difficult to imagine playing hockey to a decent standard while dressed so heavily.

Probably taken on Empire Day 1902, this picture 'For the children, the future builders of the mighty Empire' is typical of the universal belief that the Empire would last for ever: in reality, it was already in decline at this time but the glitter and pageantry of the Edwardians disguised the fact.

Violin players at the County Council School at Markyate, around 1929.

Pupils in Staverton School in west Wiltshire dig for victory in 1917: note, however, that they have on suspiciously smart clothes for such an exercise!

Chapter Four

All Change!
The Twentieth Century

*My problem all started with my early education. I went
to a school for mentally disturbed teachers.*
WOODY ALLEN

*Headmasters have powers at their disposal with which Prime Ministers
have never yet been invested.*
SIR WINSTON CHURCHILL

More variety
20s, 30s, and 40s

Primary school became more varied and fun in the
20s, 30s and 40s. Here are two excerpts taken from
the Community History Series, the first from Jackie
Bell in the 1920s and the second from Trevor Hill in
the late 30s:

'There was nature study in the lanes and occasional sports
in a nearby field. The school had its own garden from 1927;
the younger children planted bulbs and wallflowers and
the boys received instruction in pruning fruit bushes. In
the 1920s, for the Christmas concerts, the children made
everything themselves. The girls are doing fairy frocks, the
boys cardboard work, programme printing etc.
Needlework, including lacemaking, continued throughout
these years – it would take months just to make a handkerchief.'

'The main subjects were arithmetic, English, penmanship
and history. There were also nature walks and school plays.
We played cricket, football, shinty, which was a form of
hockey, and rounders'.

*'You lookin' at me?' Local lads – Arthur Vertigans, Leslie
Lingwood and Ronny Lingwood – look fiercely at the
camera in The Street, Sculthorpe, Norfolk in the 1930s.
These lads were well-known for playing tricks, such as
smoking out the village cobbler by cutting a square of turf
and placing it over his chimney pot!*

*Sir Chris Hoy would probably not have won Olympic
Gold on this spartan bicycle ridden here by a celebrated
son of Hampshire, Tommy Salter, in 1920.*

Schoolchildren dancing around the Maypole in Markyate Village, Herts, late 1920s.

The fine Heathcoat Boys' Orchestra in the 1920s with teacher, Miss Marjorie Woodward.

Riding lessons at Ryalls Court School, Devon around 1933.

Children running at St David's sports day near London in late 1930s/40s, from The Book of Monks Orchard and Eden Park.

My Mum, looking very grown-up at the age of 16, 1932.

Lady teachers are only a relatively recent phenomenon. Here are five young ladies who underwent teacher training at Itchen College, around 1916.

The Boxing Club of Mulbarton, near Norwich, late 1940s. Boxing seemed popular in Norfolk schools: my school made quite a thing of it and I was pressed to fight on two occasions when I was 16. I won the first bout, lost the second in a record time of under two minutes, and retired.

In the 1920s physical exercise for girls was fine but decorum must be kept at all times: these young ladies from Itchen Secondary School must have been sweltering in their almost tent-like outfits.

'You can breathe now, girls!' Sports day at Mylor, Cornwall, 1964.

A domestic science class at Haughley School, Suffolk, in 1940.

As the Second World War approached, schools were disrupted by the visits of air-raid wardens who gave instructions on the use of gas masks. Many schools also built trenches and a shelter. School meals and milk provision increased. Very few schools – in towns or country – escaped the chaos of mass evacuation of children. It is a sad fact that many rural schools suffered falling rolls and closed shortly after the war.

Honiton school, which we will come across in these pages several times, was one such. It was wound up in March 1947, the last remark in the school log being succinct and sad:

'21.3.1947: Class very trying this morning - the children seem more stupid than ever'.

Looking like a scene from the horror film 'Night of the Ghouls' this is, in fact, a picture of gas mask training in Addiscombe, south London, during the early years of the Second World War.

Schoolchildren were not exempt from having to wear these uncomfortable contraptions which must have been responsible for many a nightmare!

Hilda Peacock and Jean West, from Easton, between Norwich and Dereham, try on their gas masks during the Second World War.

The Gould platoon of the Junior Home Guard at the Dartmoor community of Lower Hisley in 1943.

Florrie Eales of Rattery, Devon, with two evacuees standing a little self-consciously on each side of her.

Two Land Girls plus willing helpers at Brownston in Devon.

Every little helps – children on a salvage drive organised by the WVS in war-time Tiverton.

Music practice in Seaton, Devon, 1950s.

The curriculum at Blofield School near Norwich in 1948 included beekeeping.

Outing to Yarmouth for young people from Mulbarton, Norfolk, 1948.

String lessons at Blofield school in 1986.

Religion still rules 1950s

I started my own primary education a few years later, in the mid 1950s. Nothing had changed in one important respect – religion was responsible for kick-starting UK education and it underpinned everything we did at Hickstons, my small, rather peculiar, primary school in a Norfolk village. The Reverend Quantock, already introduced, ruled over it with a robust blend of Christianity and discipline. He was a big man in a black cassock who could strike terror into us tiny ones.

It was one of dozens of English boarding schools at that time that boasted an eclectic array of pupils, all there for a fee. There were fairly aristocratic boys and girls who had failed to gain entry to a 'proper' prep school - there was, I remember, a prince from somewhere exotic (that meant, to me at the time, outside Europe) and also, I think a 'Right Honourable' someone. There were a few who were obviously nuts – one, a chap who spoke a language all his own, was later struck on the head by a 'six' at cricket as he was sitting on the boundary but it make not a shred of difference as the ball bounced off his cranium and he laughed and carried on speaking to no one in particular. There were boys and girls from very rich parents, not always the most sparkling stars in the night sky, but always worth knowing because they had lots of gob-stoppers and exotic things – one, I recall had a silver device out of which curved strands of silver wire, apparently indispensable for getting rid of excess bubbles in a glass of champagne. And then there was us – me, my brother and sister, children of parents of, ahem!, reduced circumstances. Mum got a 'pay for two; get one free' deal: being the youngest, I suppose I was the free one.

Reverend Quantock was priest in charge of the local church. All of us were expected to sing in the choir and to practice before 'prep' on Monday, Wednesday and Friday evenings and to attend church twice on

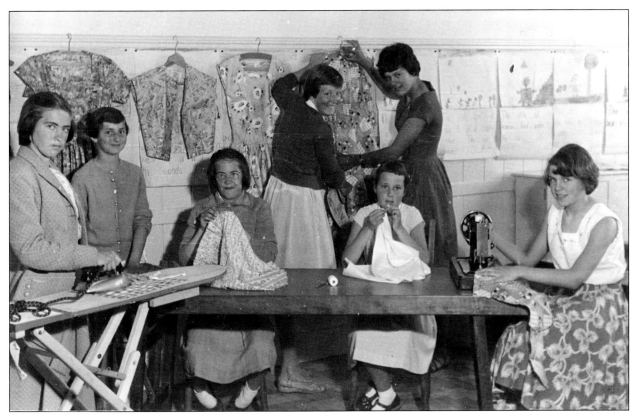

St Mawes' School, Cornwall, 1959: needlework class.

Religion still played a key role in education in the 1950s. Here is the choir of Sculthorpe church in North Norfolk, late 1950s. Often, private schools would more or less 'adopt' a local church, making choir - singing a cornerstone of the curriculum.

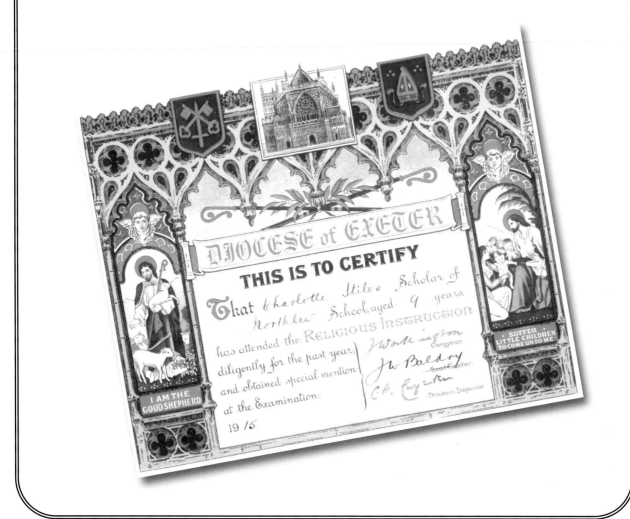

Sundays – at 11 in the morning and six at night. I remember once, standing in a line at choir practice, having to take part in a 'who could open their mouths widest' contest. I was about seven. I was overjoyed when the Reverend announced that 'Browning junior has got the biggest mouth' – it was the first thing I had ever won.

Once, when we started to sing, I was in a bit of a daydream and remember seeing a coloured shaft of light from the west window of the church highlighting a small frond as it gently billowed in the air and passed in front of us choirboys. I thought it was beautiful and followed it with my eyes. A sharp slap across my face brought me back to reality.' I won't tolerate boys who don't concentrate', said the Reverend. I remember this, I think, simply because schooldays – for us boys, at least – were, in the 1950s and 60s, more brutal in terms of discipline than would be acceptable today.

I was to leave Hickstons a few years later in somewhat dramatic circumstances, of which more later. Meanwhile, it was not all bad by any means – particularly, the friendships; the playing in the woods that were in front of the school; trying my first stolen cigarette that would not light no matter how hard I blew

Below: *Hemblington School ran a goat project in 1953 – the school's nanny goat had two kids which the children are weighing.*

Life was hard in the 1950s. Britain had to borrow money – rather than have it 'given' as was the case with the defeated nations – to survive. It was only finally paid back, with all interest, a couple of years ago. Here we see Joan Ball, Graham Ball, Ivor Parker and Derek Pride from Stinsford, Dorset on a rare trip to the seaside. A bit overdressed to really enjoy things, perhaps. Incidentally, Thomas Hardy used Stinsford as a model for Mellstock in his writings.

Butter wouldn't melt, would it? It was our family custom to have photographs taken at Christmas to send to relatives. Here I am garbed out in my Hickston's choirboy outfit, aged 11.

(my best friend, Douglas, managed to smoke it, no problem, which made me very suspicious); the excitement of my first school fete when I was put in charge of the dart board – unfortunately, on trying it myself, I missed the board completely and the dart ended up in a lady's right arm, but she was ever-so-nice about it; and the sports, as I was quite big and could run fast. I also became a dab hand at ironing as we had to look after our own shirts and trousers – at seven and a half I could put a razor-sharp crease in my grey shorts as good as anyone in Saville Row.

We all had to get fitted for the complete outfit, the bill for which would be sent to our parents: two blazers with Hickstons badge, five shirts, three pairs of trousers and, yes really, a pair of wellington boots and a black rubber mac. The reason for the latter two items was that we might have, in year two, to go from the dormitories to which we were transferred, to the main house if we wanted to go to the toilet or have a bath. It was all of five yards, but woe-betide you if you were caught nipping across the yard without being dressed like a German storm trooper.

My Mum told me, years later, that the cost of these things made her weep. She says she sat on the stairs of our Council flat – we had gone from relatively rich to impoverished when she left my Dad – and tried to work out how she could afford all this. She had a good job already, as manager of food services for Surrey schools, but she took on an extra job as a waitress in the evening at the local petrol station restaurant. One day, a neighbour came in to eat. He recognised her straight away.

'Please don't tell anyone of this', she said.

'I admire you for it', he replied.

I had my first experience of being loved at this time, tho' I didn't realise it.

One day, my desk had lots of sweets in it. Some fruit gums and a walnut whirl. The next day, even more, including fruit salads, my favourite. More of the same next day. I took them all to the teacher who gave them out among the class. I glanced around and saw a blond boy, curly haired, wearing an expression of grief. His face was wet with tears. I never saw him again. I think, maybe, he left the school shortly afterwards. We were both about nine. Sometimes, when my mind is in 'neutral', I remember him.

I only took one exam at Hickstons and that was the 11+. I can remember one question in it along with my answer. The question was:

What is wrong with the following advertisement?

'Why kill your wife with housework? Let us do it for you. Reasonable rates'

My answer: 'Some people will have the cleaning done and not pay for it'. Ah well! I was deemed 'borderline' and had to take it again. I passed this time and could thus go to grammar school.

A radical shift in perspective, 1960s and 70s

School life seemed quite simple, if quite harsh, to a child at this time. All was to change in primary education dramatically in the 1960s and 1970s as chronicled in *The Book of Pimperne, A Millennium Celebration*, compiled by Jean Coull. Here we hear from Malcom Reed, Headteacher of the Primary School from 1965.

These youngsters from Blofield School, near Norwich, look very happy with their new pool in 1961. I can remember, at about the same time, my PE teacher, a Mr George, who used to say ' Change – two minutes; side of pool – one minute; into pool – go'. Oh, the icy blast! It wasn't heated and I noted he never went in himself.

At the time of my appointment in 1965 the curriculum was still largely based on the three Rs. However, certain innovations were beginning to appear; for example, 'colour factor', a box of coloured blocks of wood, was proving very popular as an aid to mathematics. This had been introduced before my arrival and appeared such a success that Mrs Waterman and her class were often asked to give demonstration lessons for visiting teachers.

In fact, this was but the beginning of a radical reorganization of primary education. During the sixties and seventies great pressure was brought to bear on primary schools to make fundamental changes to their organization and methods. Teachers who had, for most of their professional lives, based their work on a more formal approach were now told that this was wrong. We were told that a more flexible approach was to be encouraged. Timetables were to be abolished, and the 'integrated day' and open-plan classrooms became the aim.'New Mathematics', mathematics workshops, and 'Do You Understand?' were watchwords. New reading schemes based on strange symbols were to be encouraged. Heads and assistants were expected to attend numerous courses and conferences to experience and evaluate these new methods and applications. Of course, some reacted enthusiastically, but many more felt threatened and breakdowns were common. Many eminent educationalists disagreed violently with the new theories. They published 'Black Papers', denouncing the disintegration of the education system. Some pupils responded to the approach. Two lads, after a lesson on

surveys, decided to hold their own. One lay on the pavement at the side of the road, the other hid in the hedge intending to count how many cars stopped to investigate – results not known!

The Book of Markyate by Markyate Local History Society tells us of similar changes to the idea of competitive sports in the 1970s.

….there was a 'new' wave of thinking that there should be more skills-based events and less bias towards purely competitive events. We were impressed by the way the children were involved in as many as 12 or 15 events as opposed to only 3 or 4 that was in our 'old' style. Our 'old' sports day saw most of the children sitting in their pens for the majority of the afternoon. With the new style, they spent the whole afternoon rushing from one event to the next in order to complete as many as possible, if not all, in the time allowed. That way, they could score some points. Points were awarded based on time taken or number completed rather than winning or losing. This meant that every single child received an award, based on the number of points they earned. The certificates were graded from five stars to one star. The one minor criticism of this 'new' style came from some of the parents who were used to sitting in rows and cheering the track events. We were all convinced that this 'new' system was much more demanding for all of the children who were encouraged to think, not in terms of winning or losing, but in improving their own 'PB' (personal best).

Education with a difference! Children get ready for a cycling proficiency test in Seaton, Devon, 1960.

The hoopla stall at Bransford School fete, Worcester 1975.

It is hard to doubt the sincerity of those who thought up this kind of thing, some of whom I taught with as a young teacher. The only, rather large, flaw was that children were simply not interested in getting a medal in 'Personal Best'. Children are naturally competitive and, as far as I know, the Olympics does not yet give a gold medal in 'PB'.

The great debate

My family was quite proud that I went to a grammar school – my brother passed the 11+, too, and attended the same one – King Edward VII Grammar School in Kings Lynn, Norfolk. All of us who went to school at this time, in fact at any time from the 1950s to 1980s, did so against a background of one overwhelming battle raging for educational hearts and minds. I refer, of course, to the 'grammar school/comprehensive' debate.

A few years ago, I was a guest speaker at a conference of UK headteachers. My twopence worth – a talk on how schools in different parts of the Commonwealth could help each other – had gone down tolerably well in the morning session. We were now at lunch. Now, the thing about headteachers is that they demand a good lunch, washed down with ample supplies of (Commonwealth, naturally) wine. There were close to 100 attendees, most from comprehensive schools, some from grammars and a few from public schools. A friend of mine, headteacher of a grammar school in Cheshire, came over to me at lunch – it was a buffet sort – with a sorry expression on his face.

'I don't know how I am going to keep them awake', he said.
'Oh, no, David, you mean…?'
"Yes, I have got the 'graveyard' session – first talk after lunch. They'll be fast asleep after all this wine.'
'Well,' I replied, trying to look cheerful. 'You'll just have to think up something to say that will stop them dropping off'.

Little did I know that I was about to witness an act of genius, and one of the best opening sentences I have ever heard in an educational talk.

'Good afternoon, fellow headteachers. I trust you enjoyed your lunch,' David began. ' I am going to talk to you about that kamikaze route to educational mediocrity – the Comprehensive system'.

Well, after that, wine or no, he had their full attention and the post-speech discussion was particularly lively.

I think most people would think he had a point, although expressed maybe in an extreme way. Comprehensive schools were introduced into the UK in the late 1940s – the first was Holyhead County School in Anglesey in 1949. From the beginning, a weakness was that they were not so much proposed as an attempt at hitherto unrealized excellence but more as a measure of dissatisfaction with existing secondary modern schools and the very unreliable 11+ exam. There was not much wrong with grammar schools and this is brought home by how the new comprehensives 'aped' them – gown wearing teachers, lessons conducted in formal style, school songs, mottos etc.

There was no denying the class divide that the old system exacerbated. My school, King Edward VII Grammar School, was divided from the local secondary modern by a railway line: it could have been the Berlin Wall as far as both schools were concerned, for the alien world beyond was never to be entered.

No going back

Post war experimentation also applied to buildings. My family home was in Hunstanton, Norfolk for some of my secondary schooldays and I would regularly be driven in or out of the town – 'Sunny Hunny', as us locals used to call it, more in hope than fact – past the Brutalist cubed structure that was Hunstanton Secondary Modern School, now renamed the Smithdon High School. It was built between 1949 and 1954 to a design by Peter and Alison Smithson and it was quite a startling sight for the time: steel frames exposed, everything squared, with huge panels if glass. Part of the idea was to let light flood in which was fine; only thing, according to some mates we had there, was that it became unbearably hot in summer and froze your fingers off in winter. It looked nice from the road, though, a bit like a huge modern sculpture. Maybe it was symbolic of Britain at this time – the Empire had disappeared in the twinkling of an eye, we were seeking a new world role and the old rule books for architecture, and all sorts of other things, were being torn up.

The point of no return was reached when, in 1965, Anthony Crossland, Secretary of State for Education in Harold Wilson's Government, instructed all local education authorities to convert to comprehensive education. The backlash was almost immediate and grew as poor standards appeared. As a young teacher, I remember hearing Dr Rhodes Boyson, a noted headteacher and critic of the new system, speak at a number of conferences and, although on the other side of the divide at that time, believing in liberal education for all, I was mightily impressed by his arguments for academic excellence. Margaret Thatcher tried to reverse the process when she became Prime Minister in 1979 but the situation was too far advanced for anyone to stop it. Since then, there has been a backtrack, in fact if not in theory, as the government has supported specialist schools, which promote excellence in specific specialist subjects, as well as allowing parents to choose which school their offspring attend. Sometimes it is necessary for parents to buy a house in a particular catchment area in order to send their children to the local school. These houses fetch a premium. Critics point out that this kills the idea of a 'community school for all' stone dead and, furthermore, it is now money and not academic ability, which rules the roost.

Grammar schools dominate the curriculum

I am pleased to have attended a *scolae grammaticales,* or grammar school for readers without 'O' level Latin, the first of which was King's School, Canterbury (established 597) followed by the King's School, Rochester (604). These were privately funded. The first grammar school paid for out of the rates was, quite remarkably, set up as early as 1503 – Bridgnorth Grammar School: we can only assume that there must have been some most persuasive and enlightened citizens on the council. In Wales, the first grammar school was Christ College, Brecon (1541) and James I founded a series of such schools in Ulster. These, and the vast majority thereafter, were funded by charitable bequests from wealthy citizens.

In terms of subject matter, there was only one that mattered – Latin, which, from dawn till dusk, would be taught by rote. Having taken Latin 'A' Level, which I passed at the lowest level by the sole expedient of learning huge chunks of Latin poetry and prose by heart - the meaning of which I never did, and still don't, have the faintest idea – I can only begin to imagine how hard life must have been for the schoolboys. In some schools it was forbidden to speak English at all. My kindly Latin master would encourage – 'think, boy, think!' – and only occasionally express exasperated disappointment – ' what do you mean you don't know what that word means: it is the genitive form of the nominative I instructed

you in last week!' – but the boys of the original grammars would live with the birch as a constant stimulus to their concentration.

It was only in 1840 that it became legal to divert money to the teaching of other subjects. Also, under the benevolent eye of Queen Victoria, girls came into the picture – the famous Cheltenham Ladies'College was founded in 1858 under one of the great pioneers of women's education, Dorothea Beale. Girls could now try for university.

My school: I get into trouble

King Edward VII Grammar School, my school, was founded rather later than some but had one overwhelming distinction: Royal Patronage. King Edward VII took an active interest in the place, visited it, and personally awarded a gold medal to the top boy each year. The favoured boy would generally travel to the royal residence at nearby Sandringham to receive his medal. I have been unable to find anyone who has one of these medals now but maybe an example still exists in someone's attic.

The school was ruled during my seven years by a well-meaning man who smoked constantly, called Mr Small. The tone of the school was set by the morning assembly. First would enter the boys who would sit down on the floor of the main hall. Then the masters, some in university gowns, would file onto the stage and take their seats in chairs. Finally, Mr Small would sweep in from the Head's Office, a few yards away. We would sing a hymn, receive a short address from the Head, and those boys who were to report for detention that week would be required to stand up in disgrace. That was it – we knew the assembly would not be too long because Mr Small would not want to be too long without a ciggy.

I only had to stand up in assembly once, and I can remember exactly why. I was 14 and the topic in our English class was 'poetry writing'. We had been instructed to compose a limerick for the previous night's homework. I was not the only one to have problems. Mr Halliday, our English master, asked a boy called Hawkins to stand and recite his limerick.

'I am having a problem with the last line, Sir'

'Never mind, Hawkins, let's have what you have got'.

'Right, Sir. It goes like this…I can only recite it, Sir, if Jenkins stops tittering..'

'Jenkins will stop tittering'.

> *'There was a boy all a twitter*
> *Whose role in school was to titter,*
> *I would really like*
> *Him to get on his bike*
> *And …'*

'Thank you Jenkins!' Mr Halliday raised his voice. 'That will **do**!'

'OK, thank you, Sir,' Hawkins resumed. ' The first four lines are:

> *'There was a sick man from Frome*
> *Who decided to go to Rome.*
> *His only hope was to see the Pope…*
> *That's it, Sir'.*

'Who can complete it?' Asked Mr Halliday 'Yes, Smithers, recite the whole thing with your new line'.

'Yes, Sir. Here we go:

> *There was a sick man from Frome*
> *Who decided to go to Rome.*
> *His only hope was to see the Pope*
> *But he couldn't and had to go home.'*

For some reason, I did and still do, find that incredibly funny. At the time, I was laughing so much I hardly heard Mr Halliday say:

'And now Browning – kindly illuminate this class-room with your brilliance. What limerick have you for our delight?' Needless to say, I had nothing – try as I might, and ever since, too, I have never been able to write Limericks. I did detention on the following Wednesday evening, when I had two hours to write an essay entitled: *'Is laziness the same as stupidity? Illustrate from your own personal experience.'*

My favourite subject was History. We had a very good history master leading up to 'O' levels, called Mr Worrel. We used to write essays in a special book. One day, egged on by my friend, Luis, I wrote the following in the front of the book *'Stephen Browning's Superior Dissertations in History, with select comment and evaluation by P. F .Worrel.'* He crossed it out but never said a word.

I liked the Arts but not Sciences. Smithers, referred to above, used to sit at the back in Chemistry lessons and would occasionally grunt and groan and we all knew what he was doing. He used to experiment by pouring miscellaneous liquids down his trousers. When we were fifteen, we had a new, very popular, Chemistry master, barely out of university. The experiment was to do with litmus paper, I remember, and involved turning a pink liquid blue by adding certain crystals to the mix. Suddenly there was a loud groan from Smithers. Our new Chemistry master, without looking up from his desk at the front of the class said: 'You'll burn it off, one day, Smithers. Now put it away.'

I remember the school as being traditional in approach, but this was a period of experimentation and we were not exempt. It was decided to push the top stream and have them sit exams two terms early. Consequently, we did both our 'O' levels and 'A' levels two terms early. I could not understand the point of this. 'O' levels' were OK but my 'A' level grades were inevitably lower than they could have been with more study. I later learnt that Gordon Brown, Labour Prime Minister, was also sent to Kirkaldy High School two years early on an academic hothouse programme. He wrote that he detested this 'ludicrous' experiment with young lives. I completely agree.

I stayed for one extra term to do Oxbridge Entrance. I sat it with one of my friends, Harry. The exam paper was full of strange questions, some bordering on the weird. Afterwards, I was comparing notes with Harry.

'That last question – 'What is a question?' – I spent a long time on that. I analysed all different sorts of questions – I think I did OK', I said.

'Oh, really,' sniffed Harry, 'I kept that one really short. I just put 'What is an answer?'

He went to St Catherine's College, Cambridge; I went to Kent.

So how did you do? School Reports

It is surprising how bland most school reports are. It is probably the *fear* that they may say something terrible which causes concern to the pupil. Most state the obvious , eg, – 'could do better '. Some seem to suggest that the teacher cannot actually remember who the student *is*: a lady, now in her 70s, recalls her reports for History over several years:

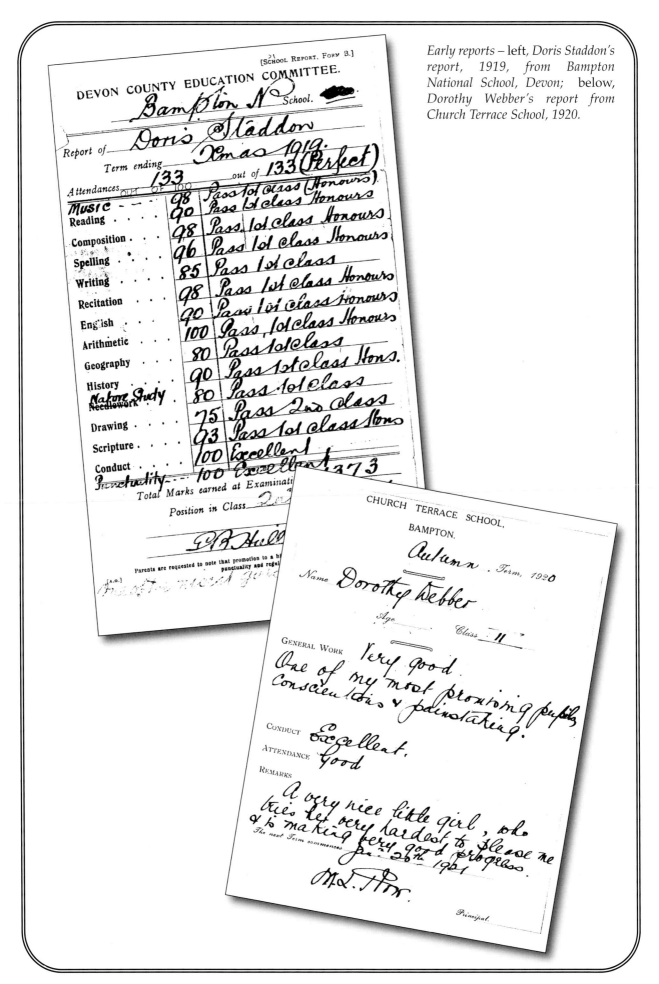

Early reports – left, Doris Staddon's report, 1919, from Bampton National School, Devon; below, Dorothy Webber's report from Church Terrace School, 1920.

A school report from Church Terrace School, Bampton, for Kathleen Webber, aged 7, dated 1920: ' A really nice girl but a bit too indifferent as to results of her work.'

'It always said 'Fair', 'Moderate', 'Reasonably good' or 'Could improve'. I am sure I was the invisible girl!'

One way to get noticed was to have an idiosyncratic trait. Johnson, in my form for History, could not write any piece of English without a howler or two. I remember he wrote that Utah was full of Morons; that St Paul got stoned because no-one believed him; that Shakespeare did not write the plays attributed to him but probably someone else of the same name; and that the Germans wanted to win the war, but couldn't, and didn't, but should've and could've but we did so they didn't (or something like that).

I can only recall one report of mine but that is because it is a gem. I think it was in the Third form at grammar school that the English teacher wrote; 'able perhaps; idle certainly'. I have always been in love with the English language and I remember marvelling at this beautiful and succinct use of words and rolling it around my tongue. The fact that he was calling me a lazy so-and-so bothered me not at all.

Teachers are also human and have written some reports that turned out to be totally wide of the mark.

The greatest leader of the 20th century, Winston Churchill, was said to have no ambition (he, himself believed that his fellows outstripped him in most regards and became quite morose at times); and John Lennon was certainly on the road to failure. Of course, some people are late developers and talent is not always apparent at school. Sir John Major, Prime Minister 1990-97, left school at 16 in 1959 with only three 'O' levels – History, English Language and English Literature, and subsequently failed to get the first job he applied for, that of a bus conductor.

Most entertaining are the reports that fail to spot someone's potential. A useful exercise I found as a teacher of creative writing to students of all ages was to write a report on someone – it can be anyone from a singer to a politician to a historical figure – where later potential is not being spotted in the classroom. These two examples are written by 6th form English students: the second one was done as a joint class exercise and is the better of the two I think as it reads more fluently and contains subtle references to Holmes' life that only a fan would spot.

SCHOOL REPORT
WILLIAM SHAKESPEARE, LOWER SIXTH

I am sorry to have to write that your son, William, is showing no promise at school whatsoever. In general, he behaves in a decidedly off-putting manner.

General communication skills. Unnecessarily ornate: he cannot say 'hello, David', but it must be 'Brave David, noble David, sweet David, thy quality precedes thee'. Some boys are beginning to shun him.

Botany. Does not have a clue: when asked by the master what he was holding in front of him (a carnation) and asked about its perfume, he replied: 'a rose by any other name would smell as sweet.'

English. Particularly poor: our long-suffering English master set the essay question 'Where would you ideally like to be right now?' He wrote ' Ah! to be or not to be, that is the question!' and promptly put down his pen.

Law. No understanding. In answer to a request to explain the jury system to his class in a few simple words, he said ' The quality of mercy is not strained: it falleth like the gentle rain from heaven.' Jones minor was heard to mutter 'what is the stupid burke going on about?'

In general his behaviour is causing alarm. Pupils of his age often suffer from acne. Matron recommends a good wash and possibly some antiseptic cream. Last night, just before lights out, young William was found in front of a mirror, slapping his face, crying 'Out damn spot, out I say!'

When asked to help lay the table for school dinner, he grabbed a knife, jumped back in horror and cried out ' Is this a dagger I see before me?'

It has been cold this term. I once saw him shivering in class and asked if he would like to put on an extra jumper before continuing his work. He fixed me with the most pathetic look and muttered 'now is the winter of our discontent'. At a loss as to the meaning of this, I looked to Smith major, sitting alongside him: ' he means it's bleedin' cold, sir.'

I am very sorry to have to write to you in these terms, but I fear that unless William can 'get a grip' as they say, his life will be one of abject failure.

Yours
James MacDuff
Headteacher

REPORT ON SHERLOCK HOLMES, LOWER FOURTH

I regret to have to inform you of some most erratic behaviour by your son, Sherlock, this term. He has always been a highly strung boy, but I am now becoming increasingly concerned. I will recount an incident this week, as told to me by his steady and reliable friend, Watson, who I think may one day become a fine doctor. It was just before the start of an inter-house football match.

'Come, Watson,' said Sherlock. 'The game is afoot!'

'No, Holmes,' replied Watson. 'It's due to start in 15 minutes'.

'It will be a draw, Watson'.

'How can you be so sure, Holmes?'

'Our forwards lack penetration. Agreed?'

'Agreed, Holmes'.

'And our defence has some very sound lads, does it not, Watson?'

'It does, indeed'.

'Then, always remember my golden rule – when all other possibilities have been explored, whatever remains, however improbable, must be the truth. Thus we will not score, nor will we concede a goal. Therefore it will be a draw.'

We lost 6-0. Afterwards, during refreshments and buns, the school cook asked Holmes how he would like his lemonade, strong or weak? 'A 7% per cent solution, if you please.' He then picked up his violin and, screeching the strings wildly, drove everyone from the refreshment tent.

Later, in the dorm, he said to me, 'Ah, Watson, how my mind rebels against all this inactivity! I may have to increase the strength of my lemonade.'

"No, Holmes, No, ' I implored him. ' Besides, surely, you are fully engaged in translating Ovid's complete works into rhyming couplets?'

'It is not enough, Watson. Luckily, I have a three-mint problem to engage me at present. Would you like to hear it?'

'I would, indeed, Holmes'.

'It concerns the curious incident of the dog in the night-time'.

'But the school does not have a dog. At night or at any other time'.

" That is the curious incident, Watson. Did you ever know a headmaster of a major public school who did not have a dog traipsing about after him – most probably a pair of Springer

Spaniels?' *The only conclusion is that he is not who he purports to be.'*

'You mean, you mean....'

Yes, my dear old friend, our illustrious head is none other than Moriarty himself.'

"Good grief, Holmes'.

He is also becoming insufferable in class. At the end of a class on Darwin's theory of Evolution, Mr Legrange, our Oxford educated teacher of evolutionary theory, asked Holmes what he thought.

" A most lucid, intelligent, logical and excellent hypothesis about how we came to be here, Sir'
'I am so glad you approve, Mr Holmes!', said Mr Legrange.

'Unfortunately', continued Holmes, 'wrong in almost every important respect.'

'But, Holmes, how can you... how can you justify such a statement?'

'Elementary, my dear Lestrange'. Here Holmes began to pace about the room, eyes flashing, arms excitedly waving, while he expounded his own alternative philosophy. The sun went down and still he talked. Everyone else had gone hours ago but he hadn't noticed.

I can only conclude that Holmes lacks any sense of reason.

Yours sadly
Mycroft Moran
Headmaster

Chapter Five

A Chapter of Schoolday Memories - Part One

school, friendships, family, special days, punishments and games

Beware you are not swallowed up in books! An ounce of love is worth a pound of knowledge.
R. SOUTHEY 1820

It should be noted that children at play are not playing about; their games should be seen as their most serious-minded activity.
MONTAIGNE 1533–1592

I loved researching this chapter and chapter 8, which continues the memories. Unless indicated otherwise, all memories are taken from the Halsgrove Community History Series.

1930s Punishments

From *The Book of Addiscombe, Volume II* Canning and Clyde residents Association and Friends

My friend, Bill Holland, upset Miss Crutcher and was hauled to the front of the class and she rapped his knuckles very hard with a thin pencil-like ruler which subsequently broke. Such was her wrath that she then picked up a round ebony ruler about half an inch thick and finished her punishment on his knuckles. He was a tough lad; he didn't cry but held it back. I don't know what he did to receive such punishment but I, at least, thought he was a hero to have endured it.

For an infringement in the playground, knocking a child's tooth out, I was told to wait outside Mr Lister's office after school hours. His office was also in the tin hut, nothing palatial for the headmaster. After hearing my pathetic story, much to my amazement, he dismissed the incident and was quite nice and charming. A child's impression of an ogre was gone.

This was how you may have travelled on the village outing in Norfolk, 1914.

A day at the seaside in Lyme Regis, 1914.

*Don't get dirty now! Children from Rattery, Devon, in their Sunday best, probably
in late Victorian times.*

Family Life

Harry Banner, born 1920, talking to
Sheila Wright in October 1989.
From *The Second Book of Leigh and Bransford*
Compiled by Malcolm Scott

'I remember, after my father had died, my mother growing potatoes and cabbages etc for the winter months by the cottage, and on a piece of land (an allotment really) at the end of the station yard. She was losing a lot to the rabbits and hares. My father had taught me how to catch them by setting a wire, so I set one and caught a great big hare. So big that, when I carried it, its head touched the floor. This was when I was a boy mind. My mother didn't think we could eat it, and said my father used to take them down to Mr Hiley, at The Fox. So I took it on my bike, and got three half crowns for it (37p). I thought I was the richest man in Leigh. Enough to buy a bag of sugar, or something more to eat than normal.

Milk was fetched from the dairy in a jug. Corn to feed the fowl, and paraffin were fetched from the shop. Everyone had their own pig, and a few fowl. We would go and catch a rabbit to supplement our diet.

On a Sunday evening we would walk down the railway line to The Fox and have a drink, and walk back along the road. The Fox was the nearest pub, but I was told that a black and white cottage at the top of the village was once a pub, called the Ring of Bells. Life was quite a struggle for everybody. My father was only 49 when he died. He had strained his heart with heavy lifting, and in the First World War he was shot in the legs. On Sunday afternoons he took the family for a walk, and I remember that there were some leaves up by the church wall which he picked and bandaged round his legs to ease the pain'.

David A Berwick is a noted Norfolk historian and author of *Beating the Bounds in Georgian Norwich*. This is the first of 3 pieces by him.

Bull Close Road Infant School 1950 – The Jackdaw incident

One day, whilst us kids were all milling about in the playground during mid-morning break, some of us spotted a Jackdaw land on the guttering of a low roof just above the school entrance. One of my little friends, (don't remember who) said something like "look at that big bird, will it hurt us?" For a reason I know not why I replied, "Oh no, it won't do that 'cos it's tame, and it belongs to me!" This kid seemed to believe me and I thought that was that, but, oh no it wasn't! When the bell was rung for return to classes this kid went to the teacher on duty, (Miss Lines, I believe) and pointed out the bird and told her it was mine! At this moment I felt I had strayed into a forbidden place in life. I had lied, and worse, there were going to be consequences, I just knew it. The teacher, who was definitely a very nice lady who I liked a lot, called me over. I should explain that, at this moment, all the kids on the playground were standing still and quietly waiting for the signal to go back into school. The teacher asked me if it was true that this bird was my pet. At this point I could easily have sorted the whole thing by saying something like, "Oh no, it isn't my pet, I actually said I wish it was." But I didn't, and went on to compound the whole thing by saying that it was mine and that it had escaped its cage this morning before I left for school. Why oh why I did this I can't even begin to explain.

It now got worse because I was asked why I had the bird in a cage in the first place. I said it was found injured by my dad, who built a cage for it to recover in. At which point the teacher, obviously utterly charmed by my story, decided to go public by shouting out the 'facts' so far to all the waiting kids. I was then invited to go forward to the bird and call it off the gutter as I said it answered to the name of 'Jacky' and would fly down and sit on my shoulder! Was there no end to my lying abilities? There was a murmur of excitement around me. I called the bird, which

Morris Dancing at Thorley School, near Bishop's Stortford, 1930s.

of course paid no attention to me whatever. I told the teacher that I thought it was nervous of all the children. At which point, incredulously, she told everyone to go in very quietly "while David waits here with me". What had I got myself into? What was going to happen next? After the throng had gone into the school the teacher said what should we do now? Unbelievably, I replied that if I walked home, I thought it would follow me as I only lived down the end of the road on which the school stood. Can you believe it? The teacher actually said "OK, you nip home now and see if it will go with you, and come straight back". So I went home where my mother was startled to see me. I had then to explain it all to her, and I don't blame her for disbelieving every word! Mum could be strict, and gave me a sound and deserved telling-off, and sent me off back to school. To my utter delight, when I got back to the playground the bird had gone! The teacher asked me if the plan had worked and I said yes, it was back in its cage, and I would make sure it was only released when it was better! Happily, nobody ever asked about the bird again, and I don't think mum told dad either!

Cricket in the 1950s

by Frederick Alan Reynolds
From *The Book of Veryan and Portloe*
Diana Smith and Christine Parnell

'Cricket was played in a field at Terwartha opposite the front of the chapel. Veryan, having the Tregunna and Kendall families and numerous others were well-blessed with very capable cricketers. An accomplished cricketer called Murphy opened the batting for Wadebridge and Cornwall for many years but as often as not Jackie Dowrick would get him out in the first 2 or 3 overs of their innings. One of my earliest memories of Phil Tregunna scoring a century, 123 if I remember correctly, in a derby match against Gerrans on a Bank Holiday Monday…

Virtually all the boys in the village learnt and played cricket … Stuart Holt used to travel from Reskivers most evenings when the weather was fine. Virtually every evening during the summer months you chased the ball from the nets until one day you were allowed to put on the pads! Later you scored for the second team every week, taking your kit, in the hope that someone wouldn't turn up. Eventually you played cricket for Veryan, and very proud you were of that achievement. It went on from there!'

Development of school uniform

The idea for the formation of a Parents' Association and for the adoption of a school uniform was born during a country dance display by the children for their parents one summer evening in 1966. A group of parents commented on how smart the children looked, particularly the boys, most of whom wore similar clothes, white shirts and grey trousers. The idea for a uniform was floated and such was the enthusiasm that a referendum was held, not only about a uniform but also about the formation of a Parents' Association. The result for a uniform was overwhelming, for a PA less so, many expressing reservations that a few strong characters might dictate policy. In spite of this we pressed ahead with both. The Managers also had reservations about a uniform; having to a man been educated in the private sector, they felt that blazers, caps an pinafore dresses might prove too expensive for many parents. They were reassured, however, when it was explained to them that more simple, inexpensive items of clothing were envisaged. In the event almost all parents adopted the uniform for their children.

I get the cane

Freddie Fox is talking in
The Book of Addiscombe, Volume II by Canning
and Clyde Residents Association

I also got the cane for taking out the sting from bees and chasing the girls with them. I put carbine in the inkwells and that made them all froth up, I had to stand in the corner and got the cane again. One boy in the classroom put a bullet in the fire and blew the fire out. The boys all had to knit for the war, helmets and gloves for the soldiers, also thick helmets for the Russians. We all used to ask the girls to help us on the difficult bits without the teacher knowing.

Picking hops

John Wenden, born 1923.
From *The second Book of Leigh and Bransford*
Compiled by Malcolm Scott

'Hop picking was an enjoyable time – I loved it. It was good to have lots of people about. They used to bring in a couple of extra policemen to the area during hop picking, due to the influx of so many people. On the first day you would arrange a price per bushel. If they thought the price was too low, they would come round the next day and stand around the back door and negotiate a better price. It was quite threatening really. It would probably be about 5-7 pence (2-3p) a bushel. Once you had set the price per bushel there wouldn't be a bad word spoken, and they just get on with the job. Some of the grandchildren of our hop pickers call by occasionally to say that this is where their grandparents came to.

My father was a rebel in 1933, when he would not join the Hop Marketing Board. He had a contract with Bass, but

Edith Thorne plus daughter at a fete in Pimperne, near Salisbury, in 1924.

A lovely picture of Mr Guest and family picking the strawberry crop at Swanwick, around 1910, with Swanwick railway station in the background. Note the youngsters, who maybe should have been in school. Some education authorities such as Cornwall realized that children would help with the crops anyway. Bowing to the inevitable, they allowed children from farming backgrounds to miss school for a set number of days each year.

had Bass turned us down we would have been on our own. We grew Goldings, which were of a high quality, and used for pale ale. Other varieties grown were Fuggles for mainstream beers, Mathons for bitter beers and Bramlings for pale ale.

Les Alford - born 1925, died 2002

'Hop picking was a fantastic time. There used to be a church service, every day at a different farm, and magic lantern shows. There were four hop pickers shops in the area, and the local people used to do quite well out of these, because the people who ran them didn't have shops back home, so they would often sell cheese and things off cheap to get rid of them. The fish and chip van came round, and a man with a bike selling ice cream'.

Games played in the inter-war years
featuring the memories of Pam Honeywill, Sally Newman, Betty Vallance, Mary Bradford and Sheila Cockings. From *The Second Book of South Brent* by Greg Wall

Their reminiscences reflect the need in those days for children to amuse themselves. They recall coming home from school and having a cup of tea, then changing and going out to play, mainly in the roads. Mary Bradford remembers

Jane Darnell of Thorley with her dolls and fine pram, 1940s.

playing donkey and two-ball on the wall outside Andrews' Fish and Chip shop. Children would skip or play with tops and hoops made by Stan Stevens, the local blacksmith. Pam Honeywill recalls playing hide and seek in Fore Street and the base (homey) was the old jubilee lamppost that stood in the centre of the junction. Mary Bradford also recalls playing with the kneelers from the Catholic Church on the grass outside. Her parents were the caretakers. Pam Honeywill and Sheila Cockings remember the concerts that children put on for their peers. They recall that one piece was a rendering of 'There I was waiting at the Church'. The audience would be charged a penny to watch, but they cannot remember what they did with the money!

Sally Newman recalls that Saturday evenings were spent at friends' houses. The children would sit around the fire whilst their parents and their friends played darts. Families would play dart and card games for amusement.

This is the second piece by David A Berwick

The happy prize-winner
George White Junior School, Silver Road, 1953

I had been ill for a couple of weeks and obviously off school as I remember watching the Coronation on our black and white tv. There were only about two other houses on Bull Close Road to have an 'H' type tv aerial fitted before ours. Quite why we were so fashionable I have no idea. My folks were no better off than many on that road, but I suspect that it was my mum who wanted to be leading the way on this occasion. For a long while after we had a tv installed we used to play host to any number of visitors. I remember the front room being filled with people, especially for the annual Cambridge and Oxford boat race. Anyway, imagine my surprise, when I got back to school, the teacher, Mr Betts, a really lovely man, made an announcement that he had got some special Coronation items to give out, but he didn't have enough for everyone. So, to be fair to us all, and to now include me and another lad who had also been away ill recently, he was going to put our names into a box and draw them out. This he did and the very last item went to me! Wow, I was chuffed. I think it was the first thing I had ever won in that manner. When I opened the rather long thin package I discovered it was a cardboard replica of the Queen's coach complete with all the horses and outriders and those walking alongside the coach. It all had to be cut out carefully, glued on the securing tabs and put together. Later, at home, this was both a challenge and a delight, as I had been a very keen cardboard model maker. There were often vans and lorries you could cut out of the back of cereal boxes. All involved very fiddly gluing and fitting, but that was what you did in those days. It was fun making things. I had that Coronation model for ages after.

Children enjoying a Coronation party, 1953.

Future schoochildren at a baby show at Pimperne, Dorset, 1947.

A pyramid display given by Seaton Youth Club in Devon to celebrate the Festival of Britain.

Mr Betts' new car

I've already mentioned my teacher Mr Betts at George White School. He has that 'special teacher' place in my memory, and I imagine many other people can likewise look back on a similar person with gratitude. It was with sadness that I heard of his passing, many years ago now. He was special because he rescued me educationally when I went into his class. I did pretty well in Class 1A but, the very next year, in Class 2A I managed a spectacular exit from A-stream standard and came one from bottom of the class. My mother was outraged at my dismal performance. My sister Margaret had always been an A-streamer and so had I until that fateful year. I was relegated into a B-stream class for the next year. The first morning that term I encountered Mr Betts as teacher of Class 3B, and from day one I blossomed again. He was such a kind and caring man and he most definitely saved me from my graceless fall the previous year. With his supporting kindness and attention to me, I regained all the confidence previously lost, and managed to finish in top place in his class at the year-end and duly went in Class 4A. My mother was pleased with

me again after the disgrace in 2A. During my very happy year with Mr Betts he bought a new car-his first I seem to remember him saying. It was a black, (of course) Morris 8. Now here's the best bit, and he would have been sacked today for doing this. A few of his 'special pupils' were given a real treat one evening after school. He drove his car onto the playground and, three at a time, he carefully drove us round the playground in a large figure of eight. It was a thrill for us kids, and, I guess, for him too. I was so fond of the man that when I eventually left that school I would go back on occasions and see him. Whatever lesson he was conducting when I entered the door, he would stop and welcome me like a returning son almost, and tell his pupils that I was one of his best ever students. A truly fine teacher, and a wonderful man too.

Games in the 1950s

Greg Wall in an article in the South Brent Parish Council Newsletter about the 1950s:

Yes, it rained in those days just as it does now, but on sunny summer afternoons we would often go down L'Aune to play in the river, or sometimes go with Miss Bessie Heard, who lived at the top of the street, out for a 'picnic' in the meadows down Somerswood Lane, or along the path fields below Aish… Then there was train spotting

A bonfire for George V's silver jubilee in 1935.

Procession in Tiverton, Devon, in celebration of George VI's coronation, 1937.

Rachel Drake with some teddy bear friends at the Teddy Bears' Picnic in Brundall and Braydeston, Norfolk, 1970.

on Station Bridge, complete with Ian Allen books. Summer evenings would see a whole group of children playing rounders or some other form of ball game in Wellington Square, using the manhole cover as 'home base' and lamp-posts and other features as the posts. I cannot even remember a window getting broken! A truce would be called if a car came by. The yew tree in the churchyard served as hiding place when necessary.

The Mummy Game

I met Julie Howitt, a singer with the band, Showbitz, when we were both guests on the 2009 Christmas special of the Maggie Secker show on BBC Radio Norfolk. She told me about the Mummy Game:

When I was a child I used to play this game which entailed wrapping my brother up in Izal toilet paper. Do you remember the cold, steely feel of it? You couldn't play this game with the modern 'supersofts'. You would start at the legs and wrap the roll round and round until, joy of joys, you were able to wrap it around his face and stop him talking. This was the first part of the fun. The second was freeing yourself by bursting out of the wrappings.

The South Brent Playgroup
Rosemary Stansbury is talking:

When we moved to South Brent in October 1973 the play-group was in the Village Hall and was run by Mrs Murphy, an experienced playgroup leader married to a doctor in Totnes. She came out twice a week to run the playgroup. I went along to see if I could help and I assisted for 2 years. She then wished to leave and felt it was time the people of South Brent ran the playgroup for themselves. I was asked to run the playgroup and, with Sue Norrish and Doreen Horan as assistants, the playgroup continued. There were normally 20-25 children, and all the equipment, including a large slide, a play kitchen and artists' easels, were stored in the basement and had to be brought up the stairs and then put back in the basement at the end of each session. The playgroup could use the Patch in suitable weather for a short session after milk and biscuits. A Rising Fives group was started once a week after play-group, run by Sue Norrish, usually for 305 children. In about 1982 I left, and Ginny Murgatroyd took over.

Evacuees
From *The Book of Hempnall* by Maureen P Cubitt

Four new children arrived from Surrey in 1940. In January 1941 there were 18 evacuees and 58 local children on the register. The newcomers had their own teachers and were taught separately. The following year the wall divid-

'I will not cry!' Croydon children were some of the first to be evacuated to safer regions in 1939.

ing the two playgrounds was taken down, allowing boys, girls and evacuees to mix at playtimes. January 1941 was bitterly cold with heavy snow. A measles epidemic brought attendance down to 17 in total. Jean Poyntz recorded the day an enemy plane flew very low and machine-gunned the school and children dived under their desks. Gerald Whiting, who remembers the same occasion, heard that the plane was shot down at Lowestoft.

Preparations for a particular family of evacuees involved renovating a cottage on the Greens and donating furniture, kitchen utensils and a pram. The family arrived and before long rumours circulated of coal being stored in the bath and good country food being shunned. That family returned to London. However, most of the new arrivals thrived. They learned how to grow vegetables and an invitation to pick apples invariably caused a stampede. They made local friends and many continued to correspond for years after the war.

Childhood Games, 1920s and 30s
Frank Palmer remembers his favourite games:

We spent a lot of time in our early childhood playing games to make up for the lack of toys and our most popular game was known as Lurky, which was a form of hide and seek. Our favourite spot for playing the game was in amongst the ivy-covered ruins, near the entrance to Court Barton Field. These ruins were the remains of the former cattle pound and blacksmith's shop. At the start of every game, a tin with a pebble in it would be placed on a large stone, near where the Coronation Tree now stands. The child nominated to do the seeking would wait by the stone for the others to hide; after successfully locating and touch-

ing a hidden child, they would then both race back to the stone and grab and shake the tin – the loser would be the next seeker.

Purdling was another childhood pastime, over the tubular railings alongside the brook near the Trooper Inn. Ropers Field was our favourite field in which to play, with the added attraction of the brook, and we used to catch minnows in jam jars and paddle in the water. Getting our feet wet was a sure way of finding ourselves in trouble when we arrived home, having defied our parents' instructions not to play in the water. The dried stalk of a hollow-stemmed plant was used for making a blowpipe, and a handful of ivy berries served as ammunition. Catapult elastic was hard to come by, and a strip of rubber from a discarded inner tube was used as a substitute. Boys also collected cigarette cards and enjoyed playing games with them. A player needed a deft flick to flip his card that much further than his opponent's, which gave him the right to have first go at throwing all the cards up in the air, and to keep all of them landing with the picture facing upwards. The boy who had thrown the second furthest would then do the same, and this would continue until all the cards had been won. Apart from a spinning top the only other toy I possessed was a metal hoop, made by the Stalbridge blacksmith at a cost of 9d. Cowboys and Indians was also played on Ropers Field, bean sticks and hessian sacks were carried to the field to construct the wigwams and we were armed with our crudely fashioned bows and arrows; it was here that many a Redskin bit the dust.

Other less physical games included searching for a four-leafed clover to bring us luck, and counting the bracts on a stem of Bennett grass whilst reciting the words of 'Tinker, Tailor, Soldier, Sailor' to try to foretell our future. Our cricket equipment would invariably consist of a rubber ball, six sticks cut from the hedgerow for stumps, and a bat hewn from a plank of wood. The smaller boys would find it very difficult to hold the makeshift bat upright; as for myself, I used to drop the bat and run to the other end whenever there was a possibility of a run.

The outside Lav

The outside lavatory was normally located at the far end of the garden and was also known as The Little Room of the Throne Room. When we were small children our lavatory always seemed a mile away from our house, and on dark nights we would only venture down there as a last resort, even when we had each other for company. We did not stop and study the stars during these times of emergency, and if an owl were to hoot our hair would stand on end. If the journey had to be taken on my own, then I would start whistling as I ventured out into the darkness, to try to

convey to any intruder that I was not afraid, although this was far from being the case. With the mission accomplished, it was a case of head down and run back to the house as fast as my little legs would carry me, bursting through the back door, and breathing a huge sigh of relief.

The following are some memories from **Maggie Secker**, who presents a much-loved programme on BBC Radio Norfolk on Sunday afternoons

I went to a little private school which was in a chapel in Hargham Road, Attleborough.

I was taken by car with either my mother or father driving. Four of us six children went to that school. The teacher was a Mrs Richmond, a strict lady but a good teacher. There were around 30/40 in the school as far as I remember - aged between 4 and 11 - all taught by Mrs Richmond in the one room. There was a pulpit at one end and at Christmas we used to have a sack in that area where children could put presents for their friends - and we all put one in for teacher - lucky lady! We had a fancy dress competition and a play every year at the end of Christmas term which was great fun.

Each school day we took our packed lunches and after we'd eaten (it was always checked that you ate everything) we went out into the playground. One of the most popular games we played was 'Fishes in the Net'. Someone would be nominated as the catcher. That person then had to run and touch someone who would then take hold of their hand and those two would run around to catch. So it went on, ending up in a long line chasing until the last one was left. That person then took over as the catcher and we'd start all over again. I do believe we did warm up exercises in cold weather before we started lessons in the mornings. During the day we would have 'Music and Movement' from the radio and also 'Singing Together' for which we had books which I imagine were obtained from the BBC. I think I still have one somewhere. There were songs like 'Drink to me only', 'Blow the wind southerly' and 'The Ashgrove'. Oh yes….and a funny one called 'Boney was a warrior' - a song about Napoleon.

On Fridays one of the older children would have to go into town with a basket to collect a hot meal from Mitchell's Bakery for Mrs Richmond. I did it when I was older. You had to walk very carefully and pay the price if you spilled the gravy!! Probably 100 lines 'I must not spill the gravy'! She regularly gave out lines. Also, if children didn't do their lines or were naughty they were rapped over the knuckles with a ruler. A list was made and first thing each morning those who were to have the ruler were called up after register as I remember.

Children arrive at the Loddiswell show in a wagon, 1971.

In the winter our free school milk bottles were put round the fire to de-ice them and how awful that tasted! Mrs Richmond would boil her milk on a free standing paraffin stove/heater and we had to watch to make sure it didn't boil over.

Having passed the 11-plus I went on to Thetford Grammar School where we travelled from Attleborough Station to Thetford on the steam train for a while and then eventually it was all diesel trains. I had a 3 mile cycle ride to Attleborough Station and then a walk of about a mile at the other end from Thetford station to the school.

I enjoyed school generally - we had a good class - very friendly girls who got on well together. We had cooked meals in the main hall which I enjoyed. We also had milk at break and could buy biscuits or Smiths broken crisps. We had excuse books for parents to sign for things like staying behind after school for tennis, late homework and missing showers etc.

My class once had a request played for us on Brian Matthew's radio programme on a Saturday morning. 'It doesn't matter any more' by Buddy Holly. That was something else! Idols ranged from Tommy Steele in the early days to Cliff Richard and Adam Faith later.

On leaving school many of the girls would throw their berets in the River Thet from the bridge as we walked from school to the station for the final time. The boys from the boys school did the same thing.

Home Food

From *The Second Book of Leigh and Bransford*,
compiled by Malcolm Scott
Cecil Dee Born 1930 is talking to Will Tooby:

'We used to keep our own pigs at home. We always had two. We sold the one which actually paid for the food for the other. A local butcher used to come round and kill them. They used to be salt-petered the same, and hung up in the house. And you'd keep cutting the bacon off until the ham and shoulders started to come together, and then you had to start to use that. But you had to have to use the bacon first, which was the centrepiece. Well you couldn't eat the good stuff until you had eaten the bad stuff!

Of course, you had your own chickens. They were always marked with little rings on their legs, to know how old they were. You used to keep them for laying for about two years. They had the knife then, and you cooked them. You knew which were coming up, you see. So you had fresh ones every year.

All vegetables you'd grow yourself – or go into a local field and find a swede or two! All local. I used to give Robertson (a market gardener down the road) all my seed in spring,

The Queen Mother arrives at St Mawes, Cornwall in 1969 to an enthusiastic reception.

Her Majesty the Queen arrives at St Mawes in 1977 as part of her silver jubilee celebrations.

and then I used to help myself when I wanted it. Well, when you were hop powdering early in the morning, a cauliflower or two in the evening didn't hurt anybody, did it? Or if you were short for bait, there was always the allotment full of onions

The Carol Choir 1920s

From *The Book of Mylor* (Cornwall) by the Mylor Local History Group. Mr Harry Moore recorded his impressions of the Mylor carol choir:

There were between 40 and 50 in the choir… On Christmas Eve, the choir journeyed to Falmouth, opened the programme at Market Strand and then toured the town, singing outside the hotels and reaching Mylor about midnight. At 7 am on Christmas morning, the choir sang in the village, then went to Mylor Churchtown, singing en route, then round Trefusis to Flushing and back to Mylor to eat Christmas dinner. After dinner we went to Restronguet and, of course, a call at the Pandora for refreshment. Then to Carclew where, after singing in front of the house, the choir was entertained to supper in the servants' hall, beer, beef pudding, cake, mince pies etc

Making the most of everything in the 1930s

From *The Second Book of Cullompton* (Devon) by Judy Morris. Mrs Marian Dummett (nee Milford) says:

In the winter our main occupation was keeping warm. At Christmas, however, we would pick holly to take indoors and always gathered a tree from the woods. One did not buy Christmas trees in those days. I can remember having a stocking with just a few little things in it, nothing like today. We always had one of our chickens for dinner and Mother would cook an ox tongue. In those days nothing was wasted. When Mr Pearsey cut off the lambs' tails and castrated the little rams we would go to the farm with a bowl and bring home the tails and the testicles which Mother would cook. I thought they were lovely then but I could not eat them now.

A Christmas party given to Norfolk children by the American airmen at Wendling Air Base, Christmas 1944

From *The Book of Wendling, Longham and Beeston with Bittering* by Stephen Olley
Birdie Schmidt is talking:

We woke up to a white Christmas Day and a heavy hoar-frost covered the ground. The fog that went with it cause the (heavy bombing) mission to be cancelled. A party had been planned for 130 orphans and refugees from Dr Barnado's Home for boys in Lexham and the Home Hale Village School children as well as those of our staff. The men on the base acted as hosts. The party was under Jane Mallory's supervision and she related how it went:

The children were taken to the Perimeter where they had the opportunity to see inside a Liberator. This was quite a

'The Royal St Omer Close Corps' made up of local Mulbarton lads, Norfolk in 1941. They either borrowed their Dad's equipment or made their own.

thrill for most of them as it was their first close-up view of an aeroplane. The GIs had their hands full in keeping order among the kids. The children were piled back into the trucks and brought to the theatre, which is next to the Aeroclub. They were greeted by the base orchestra which rendered several numbers. The children put on a programme of their own consisting of country dances, songs and recitations, and this really brought the house down. They did an excellent job and to see some of the smaller children breaking forth in song and dance, was a sight to behold. The children were shown several movie cartoons, which they just loved.

Throughout all this the children were climbing all over the laps of the GIs, and it tugged at my heart to see the expressions on the faces of the GIs. Perhaps it being my first Christmas with the GIs I didn't know what to expect, but it certainly did move me greatly to see their reactions to these underprivileged children

After the movies, the children were brought to the Aeroclub and seated at long tables in the snack bar, which was decorated with packages of candy wrapped in red paper and holly and Christmas greens placed along the tables. We served tea, cakes and fruit jelly. We had planned to have ice cream but at the last moment the freezing unit broke down. It was late afternoon so we drew the blackout curtains and lit the candles, and Santa Claus came bursting into the room, much to the glee and shouts of the youngsters. One of the GIs acted as Father Christmas and did an excellent job. He went up onto the stage where the Christmas tree stood with piles of presents stacked around it. These presents were bought with money donated by the GIs. There were 130 presents – one for each child. When we counted noses, however, we had 160 children, so we scurried around and made 30 extra presents. Santa Claus read out each name and the GIs distributed the presents. With full stomachs and full of Christmas spirit the children got back into the trucks and were taken home.

On Christmas night we played the recording of Dickens' 'A Christmas Carol' by Ronald Coleman. There was free food in the snack bar: plum pudding with sauce, fudge, nuts and apples. Lots of GIs told me it was the best Christmas they had ever spent away from home.

Dartmoor: Children play 'Happy Birthday' on handbells at Meavy in Devon to celebrate the 90th birthday of pensioner, Ethel Bowden.

Children place their offerings at the Harvest Festival in South Stoke in the West Country, c.1946.

How to make the most of a basic oven for cooking, 1920s

From *The Book of Sampford Courtenay with Honeychurch* by Stephanie Pouya
Myrtle Hunkin is talking:

We did a lot of cooking in the bread oven. We made saffron cake in it. The night before you had to chop up the saffron and put boiling water on it to get the flavour out and put all the fruit into a bowl. The next day you made your own yeast up and made the cake. We heated the oven with a faggot of wood. You had to break up the twigs small and keep on adding it until the fire had been going for about three quarters of an hour. Then you scraped it all out into the hearth. The oven was then ready to cook your yeast buns first, then your dinner, then your bread, cakes, apple tarts and pasties. You knew, as it was cooling down, the different things to put in. When that was finished and the oven wasn't too hot, my mother used to stew fruit. She would put the fruit in jars and leave them in the oven probably for hours; it would come out lovely. The oven, which was made of fire bricks, would retain the heat for a long time. We had a cloam oven at first, but them we had a brick one when that wore away. Also, if you put paper in the oven first, you could use it to air your clothes.

As part of my research into education in other countries, I have often travelled abroad. Here, four children in Canton, China put on an enchanting dance of welcome.

1978 display of girls' needlework from The Book of Blofield and Hemblington, *which is seven miles from Norwich, Norfolk.*

A beautiful wall hanging made by the ladies of Pimperne in Dorset, 1992, depicting some key aspects of village life over the centuries including schooldays, church life, farming, football, the pub and cricket.

Chapter Six

Remembering Our Teachers

*'It is when the gods hate a man with uncommon abhorrence
that they drive him into the profession of a schoolmaster.'*
SENECA

*He must have known me had he seen me as he was wont to see me, for he was in
the habit of flogging me constantly. Perhaps he did not recognise me by my face.*
ANTHONY TROLLOPE 1815–1882

The 'public' side of schooldays

Prince William and Prince Harry had it considerably easier than their counterparts of old when they went to Eton. In Elizabethan times, pupils rose at 5 a.m. and began work at 6. It was the same at Westminster. The first lesson could last as long as five hours. These days, Eton divides its day into 'schools' (periods) as follows:

7.30 – 8.15	1st school
8.15	breakfast
9.20	chapel
9.40	2nd school
10.30 – 10.45	break
10.45	3rd school
11.55	4th school
1.00 pm	lunch
3.30	5th school
4.15	tea
5.00	6th school
6 – 6.45	private study
7.45	supper
8.00	prayers
8.30	study
10.00	lights out

Public schools have always been a miniature world and reached their most powerful in Victorian times. In this mini-universe the Head is supreme – 4 Headteachers in the 1900s later became Archbishops of Canterbury. Masters and assistant masters taught classics and came from Oxbridge, as no-where else was considered to guarantee suitable pedigree.

Tyrants and fags

The public schoolboy structure was hierarchical, too. Prefects did as they pleased and made up all sorts of rules – only prefects were to wear towels around their necks after cricket; no junior boys could walk on the south side of the main quad; only Latin was to be spoken on the way to chapel on Sunday morning and so on. Fags – junior boys, who often led lives of abject misery, cold and hunger, did their bidding.

In the 18th and in the first half of the 19th century, older boys really acted out life as tyrants. They went hunting, poaching, cock fighting , badger baiting, cat and duck killing (by dogs: 'let's see how long it takes – wager anyone?') and racing and were often drunk in and out of school. Harrow boasted the 'Red Nightcap Club', dedicated to 'drunkenness and dissipation'. They could flog and bully both younger boys and any member of the public of any age almost to their heart's content. Occasionally people died but it was in no-one's interest to properly investigate the matter. Heads turned a blind eye – the so-called 'Great Rebellion' at Winchester in 1793 was against 'spying' by the Head: that at Harrow in 1808 against the proposed restriction of 'flogging rights'. Old boys were very sentimental about their schooldays – no doubt forgetting the early years of pain in favour of the later years when they were all-powerful – and resisted any ideas of reform.

Hierarchy and class

The curriculum was similarly hierarchical – literature was at the top and science at the bottom. From the mid 1850s the arts were supplanted at the top of the 'pyramid' by sports – especially cricket, football, rugby and rowing. Loyalty to both a school and a team blended well into service for Queen and Empire and led to a dangerous contempt for academic boys, a trait not entirely eliminated to this day. Young men with a public school background could hardly wait to obey Kipling's tosh and 'Take up the White Man's Burden', rushing to serve in the Great War 1914-18: Rugby lost 686 boys at this time and Malvern 457.

The Royal Commission of 1861 examined the curriculum of nine elite public schools. It ruled that there would be no inspection of such schools as this would 'degrade' them – hence they had carte blanche to do whatever they wished.

The school you attended in Victorian England told everything about your class and place in the scheme of things. There were the top schools, the likes of Eton, Harrow, Westminster and St Pauls and below these, in a carefully calibrated system came the others, some of which were founded now, often by subscription. Thus we have Cheltenham College – no families of tradespeople, please. For families of doctors, clergy, solicitors, senior Army personnel and the vast Indian Civil Service there was Marlborough and Epsom. To enter Lancing College in Sussex you just had to be rich; for Hirstpierrepoint, the son of a 'higher' tradesman – siblings of 'smaller' tradesmen, please apply to Ardingley; for Wellington or Sandhurst, the sons of serving serviceman. If Roman Catholicism was important to you, Ratcliffe and Beaumont awaited; non-conformists would probably be happier at Leys or Taunton. And so it went on.

Top girls' schools also made great progress during this time, often due to the tenacity of great educationalists like Dorothea Beale. A famous politician called educated women 'most disagreeable creations', a sentiment echoed by many. Nevertheless, in the mid century came the foundation of schools like Bedford College and Anglican Queens. In 1850 the North London Collegiate School for Ladies and the famous Ladies College, Cheltenham were founded. They were widely ridiculed – was it not obvious that Shakespeare was only suited to boys? Nevertheless, a Girls' Public Day School Trust was launched in 1872 and by 1891 had control of 36 schools. Perhaps the most famous girls' school of all time, Roedean, came into being in 1885 and tried as far as possible to 'ape' boys' public schools in organization and curriculum.

Latin and God

And what was the public school curriculum in the 1700s and 1800s? In a word, Latin - *still*. At Eton, no English, Geography, History or Maths was taught in the first year – only Latin grammar. Later you would go on to Latin fables and poetry. The kindly Charles Wordsworth, nephew of the poet, also taught Greek grammar at Winchester but the text books were all written in Latin. Help!! By the time he left, a boy at such a school could talk in Latin and had, conservatively, made up during his schooldays, many thousands of Latin verses. Some could even quote whole Latin plays without a single mistake. All of which, when they came to make their way into 18th and 19th century society, was completely and utterly ... *useless*.

Other schools tried different things. Not surprisingly, given that religion was the original engine that kickstarted schools of any kind way back in the 5th century, this was seen as something worthy in which to immerse young minds. John Wesley is reputed not to have allowed any holidays or any time off for any reason, nor any games or play at the school he founded. From early morning to late at night, the boys prayed and studied the scriptures. John Wesley was overjoyed when, as often happened, the boys broke down in distress and prayed aloud for mercy, convinced that they had found the Lord. It doesn't take a modern psychologist to recognize the signs of religious hysteria and to realize that the poor mites were praying for mercy to someone much closer to home.

The greatest-ever Headteacher?

Some learned men did, it is true, see the daftness of it all and became very angry. One such, who also changed the system for ever, was Thomas Arnold. He led Rugby School from 1828 to 1841. He has both a real and a literary persona, often intertwined, as he was immortalized in *Tom Brown's Schooldays*, a book that fizzes with life, laughter and a wholly convincing account of adolescent struggle. It had a profound and lasting impact on the way young people thought about duty, friendship, love and adults – Tom Brown was the Harry Potter of the Victorian age. Arnold, the revered Dumbledore of the 1900s, is credited with establishing a broader syllabus, of some practical use and also incorporating games (Tom Brown's moment of greatest fulfilment is not during some triumphant rendering of a Latin or religious verse but playing cricket for his school – an obvious analogy for hitting England's enemies for 'six' on behalf of his Queen). Arnold organized his school on the prefectorial system and instilled a deep sense of school pride in a boy. He was largely responsible for getting the public school system to pick itself up by its bootstraps and become what was, and still remains, a fine introduction to life for the more privileged. Marlborough, Wellington, Clifton, Haileybury and many lesser lights all subsequently recruited Heads trained under Arnold. He died unexpectedly of a heart attack at the age of 46 leaving his great 'opus' – Roman history in three volumes – unfinished. He was not celebrated overmuch during his lifetime but, within a few years of his untimely death, became one of the great Victorian heroes.

C.J. Vaughan, his protégé and successor, carried on the good work. However, he lacked Arnold's balance and sense of judgement – as an example, he dictated that the prefects should run the school pretty much on their own and only refer 'moral' matters to him, resulting in considerable chaos and mayhem. We can almost hear Arnold remonstrating with the new Head from the grave: 'But my dear Vaughan – these are still BOYS – let them be.'

Other Heads and masters – the good, the not so good and the completely insane

Being largely unaccountable to the world outside, it is not surprising that there are so many colourful, bizarre and downright sadistic masters and headmasters to be found in public school history. There was no recognized set of attributes for a good master, nor anything approaching a standard method of selection. Schools made their own requests. Common ones were that a man be not a common gamester, a frequenter of low drinking establishments, a vain dresser, a whorehunter, licentious in living, given to (unspecified) notorious vice, infected with any loathsome disease, nor a user of tobacco. On the credit side, it was helpful to be a man skilful in Latin and Greek, a good Poet, of sound Religion and, if he did not share the views of the government in the matter, to be skilled at keeping his own counsel, not under twenty five years of age, of a profound demeanour, adept in honest and sober conversation and strict in discipline.

The rewards could be great in financial terms but you had to be smart in order to get the pick of the jobs. A master of a major grammar or minor public school in the 16th century could demand £14 or £15 a year – a lot of money, but that was not all. Parents would pay the Head or senior Master a handsome premium to accept their children if the school was a good one; the Head could offer to specially 'look after' their darlings for another payment; and guess who decided which pupils got distinctions in exams? Fagging was another terrible worry for young boys, some of whom almost died from malnutrition – the likes of Flashman of Tom Brown fame would delight in making their starving fag throw perfectly good beef into the pig bin after the bullies had had their fill, leaving nothing for the poor fag but a slice of stale bread and a beaker of weak beer - and beatings. Again, the Head was in a position to put the boy under the protection of a trusted and honest senior – for a modest consideration, naturally. One Head in the 17th century was reported to have put away £60,000 before his retirement, which would make him a multi-millionaire today.

Anything to get the job

All sorts of skullduggery can be discovered in the records as men sought to gain a good position. A bribe of £10 was enough in one case in the 1600s to get the main contender to withdraw his application for a classics post in a north of England Public School. The governors of a school in Lincolnshire a century later held an 'auction' for the biggest bribe from two roughly equal contenders for the position of Greek master – it reached£40 and a cask of port before one applicant barricaded himself in the schoolroom. He got the job: initiative rewarded? One applicant for a post as Latin master in Sussex in 1870 published an article claiming that his opponent was seen tottering about the streets of Chichester in a not entirely sober state in the week prior to interview. In a case of strange poetic justice this backfired as the Bishop of Sussex considered it not beyond reason for someone under the duress caused by attending such an important interview to gain some comfort in this way. Besides, the man concerned attended the interview in a smart and sober state, no doubt liberally quoting Ovid. He was appointed.

The importance of a prized Mastership was highlighted at the top schools by a welcoming ceremony where the new teacher would be greeted by the assembled school, maybe in Greek, and be expected to give a Latin oration in response. The headboy would pledge good behaviour and obedience from the scholars (sometimes this did not last very long, but the thought was there).

Some masters were kind, one being William Wordsworth's nephew, Charles Wordsworth, Headmaster of Winchester in the 1840s: he used to give favoured students cream cakes as a reward for good Latin and Greek. The kindest master 'of all time' is reputed to have been Reverend John Smith who taught at Harrow from 1854 to 1862 and believed that God's love should always be shown: he sadly died in a mental home. Some were advanced for their time: Richard Mulcaster, Master of Merchant Taylors School for 25 years in the 17th century, pleaded unsuccessfully for the English tongue to be given precedence over Latin.

Fear and floggings

The unsaintly predominate in the records, however, and one has to question the mental states of more than a few. Nicholas Udall is known as the author of the first English comedy but there was nothing funny about his tenureship of Eton from 1534 to 1541. A violent flogger by any standards, he would sometimes teach a new boy a lesson by giving him fifty strokes for the most trivial infringement. He ended up in Marshalsea Prison for gross immorality. Robert Crayford, who ruled Perse School in the 1650s used to pick up boys by their ears and sometimes beat them literally senseless. Others who liked to lift boys by the ears in the 18th century are William Birch of Rugby, William Page of Westminster, the notorious James Boyer of Christ's Hospital, and his successor, Edward Rice, both of the latter being recorded as hitting boys so hard that they ended up half way across the room. Rice was to hang himself within a week of his retirement.

Richard Busby was Headmaster of Winchester for an incredible 57 years in the 17th century and believed that talent could primarily be drawn out of a boy by flogging, an attitude by no means unique – even students believed it. Sir Christopher Wren, architect of St Pauls, was among his pupils and sixteen of his charges became bishops. He is reputed to have refused to remove his hat when Charles II visited the school as it would have been undignified for a man in his position so to do: he must have had considerable influence to have got away with that one!

There are several candidates for the most reckless flogger of all time – one of them is Alexander Gill, Senior Master of St Paul's, infamous for taking the birch to his own grown up son – after graduation - for sloppy grammar and to sundry adults who annoyed him in the street. Another is George Heath,

Headmaster of Eton at the end of the 18th century who once gave 52 boys a dozen strokes each, although he seems to have overdone it when he birched 70 boys in succession – he was laid up in bed with aches and pains for a week and we can only imagine the sniggering and satisfaction of the boys. The most infamous Headmaster of all time, however, is most probably Dr John Keate, who ruled Eton for 35 years shortly after the retirement of George Heath. There was apparently no end to it – it mattered little if you were the perpetrator or not of any offence, or even if, when one had been committed, you were the culprit – he was known to have flogged an innocent brother on some occasions, quite aware that it was the wrong sibling. His face would become red and veined before a flogging; sometimes he would dribble and make curious animal noises. Despite all, he could not always keep order – the boys thought up many ingenious ways to confuse him in class, sometimes singing in different parts of the room at the same time - a sort of early quadrophenia - screwing his desk shut, throwing stones at him or placing a rotten egg on his seat. Questions were raised about him at Cabinet level so strange were the stories emanating from Eton during his term of office.

In my own small way, I can empathise with this situation. At Hickstons, caning was a common event. One time – I was about nine – I had cheeked a prefect. I had been playing cricket *inside* the school. The prefect, Jones, caught me.

'That is reprehensible (*what did that mean? Good or bad?*) behaviour, Browning. You are behaving very badly' (*Oh!*)

I had recently been reading about Winston Churchill and was inspired to paraphrase one of his best lines.

'But you are an idiot, Jones. Tomorrow, I shall behave well again'.

Well, caning always took place in morning prep, before breakfast. My brother, Nigel, was mistakenly called for the cane. I had half a hope that he would take my punishment. Alas, no. I got six on my bare backside.

Secondary and grammar schools - 'some unusual...

Grammar schools took their cue from the public sector. Their main subjects had always been the classics but they quickly loosened up to a greater or lesser extent. They, and the thousands of private secondary schools that sprung up, especially in the later 1900s and early 20th century, did all sorts of things. This was still a time when anyone with half a crackpot theory could set up a school. Thus we have some elysian academies where multiple languages were taught; a school just studying the 'Arts' – poetry, painting, sculpture, colour and form; the opposite, dedicated to Prince Albert's vision of excellence in design and manufacture of saleable products – when I came across this example in a book during my research, some wag had scrawled ' technical college on steroids?' in the margin; even a few with a syllabus preparing boys and girls for life of responsibility and service in the Empire for, as everyone knew at the time, this would never end.

...and some more mainstream

More mainstream, if still unusual, were schools like Abbotsholme in Devon where pupils returned to the simple life – good health, exercise and home-grown vegetables. Bedales was similar but co-educational. Oundle, from 1892, specialized in creativity and making things. Perse School in Cambridge promoted, in the school prospectus for 1902, a 'learning must be fun' approach with map and model making, theatrical productions and Morris dancing. Many of the best redefined 'practical' subjects, coming quite close to our current national curriculum, to include Mathematics, Science and English. On top of this they tried lots of new things – share dealings, land management and company sales between boys and girls; trials by pupil juries; and micro/macro economic theory. Hazlewood School in Birmingham aimed to promote the noble art of making money – there was a token school coinage, boys' bank loans, bankruptcies – this would land you in detention. Smart dress and punctuality were vital. Instead of the birch, boys would sit in a dark cupboard (I am not sure where this bit fits into the business model, though).

The monitorial system

Teaching methods have been varied throughout the ages. Flogging, as a method of driving facts into a child's brain was once universal and is, mercifully, no more. Another 'method' that was once seen as the saviour of education and which has totally vanished is the 'monitorial system'. This was championed at the beginning of the 19th century by two gentlemen, Dr Bell and Joseph Lancaster and, for several decades, was seen as nothing less than the complete solution to schooling for the lower classes. Each class needed only one skilled master – all other 'teaching' could be done by 'monitors', ie bright students who would instruct the others. Two major advantages delighted the powers-that-be. Firstly, classes could be of any size whatsoever – hundreds, maybe (and this would increase the fee of the master so no objections in that department). Secondly, teaching would have to be simple, with nothing that required discussion or debate, thus ensuring that the poorer classes were not taught anything that might – heaven forfend! – raise them up from their rightful God-given place in society which was right at the bottom. It is hard to understand today the terror that the middle and upper classes went through at the thought of a man who was a natural tiller of the soil wanting to read a book or debate current affairs. The French Revolution was on everyone's mind and the hero of the age, His Grace the Duke of Wellington, was the leader of those who feared that the uneducated soldier – the very men who had decimated Napoleon's armies – could one day turn against their rulers.

The monitorial system was abandoned after a few decades as it was seen as a good thing for all children to think a little. Secondary education was, however, piecemeal and erratic in nature until the end of the First World War. Most children still left school before their early teens: the very lucky ones would attend either a good private school or one based on the grammar model.

Headteachers get into scrapes, too: (i) The Commonwealth thing

I think teachers and heads are brilliant. In this country, as opposed to many others, they do not get the recognition they deserve. Yet, these are the most difficult jobs in the world: you are always on show, and you make a real difference. So I say 'hurrah to you'.

Whenever we think of people getting into scrapes in education, we always think of the pupils. It is not always so – one of my jobs for some years was to help resolve things when teachers and headteachers got into difficulty – usually in an overseas country.

My particular field has been Commonwealth education – assisting teachers in any way I can spend time in one of the 50 plus countries that make up this unique and wonderful organisation. The idea is to gain experience and share what is best in educational practice for the benefit of the teachers themselves and schoolchildren in all countries.

In my time, for my sins, I have worked with, interviewed, been to conferences with, hosted, befriended or spent time with many thousands of teachers and heads from all over the Commonwealth. Some cope when they come to the UK, some don't. And vice versa. Flexibility, a positive attitude and a sense of humour are vital to success in a new country; above all, as I often used to say to people, when in a new land, don't judge everyone by the one rude person you encounter in that land – there is always going to be one, probably at least a few, and you are like as not going to be tired and disorientated anyway.

Some experiences have been a bit sad, some funny and others instructive – 'I have come to England from Quebec and I refuse to exist without a microwave oven'; or 'I have been here for over a month now and I haven't yet met the Queen'. Once I had to meet a teacher from a small African state to help him get to his UK accommodation. I met him at Bond Street tube and aimed to put him on a train at Waterloo, as his UK posting was in Hampshire. We met, but Jonas – such was his name - was very nervous and fainted in my arms. I had to carry him virtually all the way to Portsmouth. He had simply never seen so many people in his life as he came up the escalator at Bond Street – we nipped into Oxford Street to pick up some supplies - and the experience was overwhelming. He got used to life here pretty quickly after that and we often laugh about what happened.

Sometimes things were simply human: ' I am in New Zealand and I miss my Mum and Dad – please can you communicate with them and tell them how much I love them?' Again, it takes a lot of courage to come to a so-called 'affluent' country on a lowish salary from, say, the African Continent – there were times when teachers could not afford to go home for holidays or even telephone their loved ones: we would often have a whip-round for a phone card. Then there were daft situations : one Englishman got lost in the Australian Outback and telephoned me from Stony Rock or somewhere – he was worried his wife would desert him (though he had found a soulmate with whom he had fallen in love). Would his wife understand? Could I, please, negotiate?

There have been some genuinely sad times, too, of course, such is life but, on the overwhelming whole, I have admired the resilience, positivity and humour of teachers and heads who choose to spend time in another country. The Aussies were particularly positive – they would generally just get 'stuck in' no matter how bad things appeared to be. (Unfortunately, this also applied to their Test team and, loving cricket myself, I suffered much humiliation during their ritual slaughter of England. They took no prisoners. One or two would phone me at work to either tell me the score or, much worse, ask me if I knew what it was ' as my radio has gone down, mate'. I had one glorious summer when the tables were turned – Oh, Botham and Willis, you will always have a place in my heart!)

These experiences date back to the previously discussed League of the Empire, founded in 1896. There seems to be a welcome shift nowadays in the way we view the previous Empire: there are undoubtedly some excellent by-products.

(ii) Stuck up a mountain

Christmas could be a lonely time for teachers and heads from the overseas (first, Empire, then Empire and Commonwealth, then UK Commonwealth and now we must be careful to say) Commonwealth, and we would often take a trip with anyone who wanted to come, spending a couple of weeks somewhere nice.

It was Christmas Eve in Romania, 1970s. I was co-organiser, with a headteacher from Surrey – of the host school of my friend, Jonas, above, actually - of a skiing trip. I didn't ski, and neither did she. She, Jane by name, was inspirational and had a positivity I had never witnessed before – virtually all her staff had experienced teaching children in Africa, New Zealand, Australia, Canada or the West Indies. Disruption to her school? Not a bit of it. Trouble with parents? What an incomparable education your children are having here! Problems with educational bureaucracy about costs? Please do come to my school and discuss this with me (they never dared). Her school was permanently oversubscribed.

We went up on the ski-lift (no skis), just to see 'our lads and lasses' go off. It was lovely getting there and watching the teachers whooshing off down the slopes. Problem was, when they had all gone we went for a stroll in the idyllic surroundings at the top of the mountain which was not a very sensible thing to do – we both missed the last ski-lift down. There we were, stuck up the mountain – what a lovely view! – with no path down. We could see the hotel below with all the pretty lights. Oh! So far away.

The sun set. There was the sparkle of the fantastic winter ice-scape, and, I remember, the clearest air and brightest stars I have ever seen. But I thought we were going to die. I looked at Jane. Her eyes were cold but brilliant blue. She was freezing, thrashing her arms around her, with her teeth chattering. But there was a vibrancy about her, almost as if part of her were enjoying this.

'We are both going to die up here, you know'.

'What is your most beautiful memory?' she asked

'Here are you , I shivered, ' up a mountain, about to die, asking me for my most beautiful memory! Anyway, what's yours?'

'Oh, I have a couple. When I insisted Charlie Jackson stay at my school, despite him having set fire to the canteen.'

'Is that the Charlie Jackson who is now a guitar star?'

'Yes. And when I accepted my beloved's hand in marriage. And this.'

'THIS?'

'Sure. How many people experience this kind of thing – the stars, the cold, the clarity it all brings?' And it gives you a chance to think... you know... what your last thoughts might be... at the end, so to speak.'

My frozen lips widened to a smile. 'Dear Jane, I would have you know that my 'last' memory is not at all noble: I am thinking about all of our party in the warm down there, enjoying dinner... .'

'Well, there's only one thing for it...'

She suddenly stood up, ran full throttle to the edge of a crag and with a loud 'Wheyyyyyy…' jumped off.

There was silence for what seemed like ever. Surely she was dead.

Then, from a long way, I heard a faint voice :' I landed in snow. Come on'.

I took a deep breath and flung myself off, too. The landing was soft. We scrambled around the mountain from that point and managed to get home.

We attended the Christmas celebrations, although we missed dinner. 'Where were you two over dinner?' asked a chap from Kenya.

'Oh, err, we had a lot of paperwork to catch up on' I said sheepishly. 'Let me buy you a Christmas drink...'

(iii) The wrong side of Paddington

One time, I was just about to enjoy Sunday Lunch when I got a call to say two headteachers from Canada had been arrested for trying to steal a car in Mayfair. 'Get to the Old Bailey tomorrow at nine sharp!' I did.

We had appointed a top barrister of the time who made me nervous as he only got there with ten minutes to go before the hearing. And he knew nothing about the case. What happened next stunned me – some people's mental apparatus works quicker than others.

He took details from the 'accused' and said to me 'it's over' (*What?…*) Then he rushed off to get dressed in his wig etc.

In court he had one (of two) policemen on the stand. He insisted they did not hear each other's evidence, so one had to wait outside.

'What was the colour of the car in question?'

'It was green, sir'.

'How did you see this?'

'Because of the lights, sir. In this part of Mayfair Avenue, there is very good lighting'

'And what did the accused do, constable?'

'They both went around the car and one of them tried the door in an attempt to steal it'

'And what was this car, constable?'

'It was an Aston Martin, Sir. I wouldn't mind it myself!'

Guffaws in court.

'You are very sure of this, Constable?'

'Quite sure, your honour.'

'I am not your honour, but we will let that pass. Stand down'.

He left the courtroom. The other policeman came onto the stand.

'Your colleague has witnessed that you saw these two gentlemen – headteachers from Alberta, no less, try to steal an Aston Marton from Mayfair Avenue. Do you agree with him?

'I do, sir'.

'And what did you see?'

'I saw one of them – the one with the moustache in the dock – try the driver's door.'

'And what colour was the car?'

'It was…err, silver'

'Silver, really? And how did you see this?'

'From the lighting in Mayfair Avenue, Sir.'

'You could see quite clearly?'

'Quite, Sir'

'This is very important. Think clearly. Are you sure you saw QUITE CLEARLY?

'Absolutely, sir.'

'Well, would it surprise you to know, constable, that the light in THIS PRECISE spot on the night of the alleged offence were out of order. How could you see?'

'I wasn't aware of that, sir'

'How far away were you?'

'About a hundred and fifty yards, sir'

The barrister went for the kill 'Here we have your colleague saying that the car was green and you say it was silver, and yet you admit there was no adequate lighting in this part of the road. This is ridiculous! I call on Your Honour to dismiss this case!'

A few minutes. 'Case dismissed!'

The Barrister was not quite finished:

'And costs, Your Honour', he sniffed, 'for the good reputation of these two excellent gentlemen. May I ask for £250,000.'

'Hmm… Yes, costs of a quarter of a million pounds awarded against the police'.

Then, this unknown barrister swept out of court. I was flabbergasted – I had seen barristers on TV, but never thought I would see one in action. He charged a substantial fee. But, My God, was he good!

(No, of course they didn't: they had had too much to drink or were, as we used to say, a bit the wrong side of Paddington, and were simply looking at a lovely car. They did touch it, though, it can now be revealed.)

I got a pint of Guinness out of it, at the pub outside the courtroom.

Chapter Seven

School Life

But there was another advantage to being elected President. The day after I was elected, I had my high school grades classified top-secret.

RONALD REAGAN

Learn to write well, or not to write at all.

DUKE OF BUCKINGHAM
1648–1721

Bringing the fashionable to the suburbs

In the 1920s and 30s, great changes were afoot. Social distinctions became blurred. Nowhere is this better illustrated than in an entertaining book *'Something in Linoleum'* by Paul Vaughan (Sinclair-Stevenson 1994) which takes us on a journey to Raynes Park County School, opened in 1935 and run by John Garrett. If, like me, you wonder what the title is all about, I can say that the author's Dad was a successful business-man who dealt in linoleum and one of the funniest parts of the book is when he volunteers to give a talk on making the stuff to his highly embarrassed son's form.

John Garrett was a product of Oxbridge and a friend of the fashionable and famous. He knew AL Rowse, WH Auden, TS Eliot, Cecil Day Lewis, the Messels and the Redgraves and he brought to this suburban part of London an eclectic and high flying group of teachers including the novelist, Rex Warner and the painter, Claude Rogers. The message was clearly that the finest minds were not wasted among the children of the more 'ordinary' schoolchildren of suburbia. This was the fresh idea of a great headmaster – if not as good a teacher of his beloved English Literature as he would have liked to be, according to Mr Vaughan's book – as well as a brave one 'ahead of his time': he came out as a homosexual shortly before his death at a time when it was dangerous to do so.

My own Headmaster

My own Headteacher, some years later in the 1960s, at King Edward VII Grammar School, probably shared many of the same values although not the long list of celebrity friends. Mr Small was quite an imposing figure to a young boy. He always seemed a bit remote as he swished by in his black gown, wisps of grey hair protruding from a large head. And he always smelt of No 6 which was not surprising as he was always smoking – not in the school corridors or classrooms, of course, but a smog hung around his office and many a boy was dispatched down the road to Gaywood tobacconist for supplies.

My friend, Philip, was daft enough to get caught smoking behind the biology lab and was ushered into the Head's office for the cane. Caner and caned could hardly see each other for the fug and the last sight Philip had of Mr Small following a half-hearted 3 strokes – for he was a kindly man and probably not unaware of the comedy of the situation – was of the Head flipping open the blue and white pack for another nicotine top-up.

A politically incorrect view of cool

We all smoked, of course – at one time or another you gave it a go. You could hardly hold your head up if you were 14 or over and did not. What we boarders did in our fourth year was establish a short-lived 'club': at 10 to four we would nip into town to a coffee bar where a coke would be bought – probably one between three. Our main purpose was to smoke as many cigarettes as we could in the next hour. I remember No 6, sharp and acrid and not very cool. Embassy were bigger and milder though not very cool either. Philip, he who got caned in the smog (how cool was THAT?) would languidly produce something exotic – maybe Three Castles or Passing Clouds, oval in shape with no filter, Woodbines or plain Players. One day to stunned disbelief he produced Black Russian, other times Gauloises – this was apparently the reason the French were great lovers - mentholated St Moritz which tasted like toasted peppermint or, to top it all, Sobranie Cocktail, fluorescent turquoise and pink with gold filters. We would sit and smoke and be cool. I did not really see the point as, like Bill Clinton, I did not inhale simply because I did not know that this was what you were meant to do: there may have been a tremendous fug but I doubt anyone else knew what they were doing either. At 5.10 we would rush back to supper which was at 5.30, followed by prep at 6. We must have smelt like ashtrays and looked a bit ashen but I cannot remember anyone challenging us, although I do recall feeling a bit ill sometimes but Philip assured me that this was because I needed more practice. And Hey-Ho, next day we were at it again. Our 'smoking club' did not last very long, though, as it was simply too expensive and, besides, exams loomed.

Some boarders, when they were prefects, used to also smoke on the school roof, or so I am told, not having been guilty of that particular misdemeanour myself. Apparently they would sneak from their beds into the main hall and get onto the roof via one of the stair turrets – the one on the right as you are looking at the stage as a matter of public information– and via the then Geography room. Nobody ever caught them and, to this day, I am not sure if that the masters knew.

And the masters...

The masters were, on the whole, a conservative lot. Mr Halliday, our English teacher and he who gave me detention for not producing a limerick, was a kindly man on the whole who, until the end of his life, took a keen interest in the school. He supervised the under 15s football team in which I, being well over 5 ft tall and quite a bruiser, played at centre forward. One day I missed a sitter of an open goal and, afterwards, Mr Halliday came up to me and said ' Don't worry – you must have washed your feet last night and can't do a thing with them today!'

Mr Knight, Head of Mathematics, had a daunting exterior and for years wore the same gaudy tie – blue with red zig-zags on it - but it was easy to sidetrack him onto rugby football which could, with skill, take up the better part of a period. He had eight daughters by the time I left the school, about one a year. He was reputed to be desperate for a son and heir but we were too nervous to mention it directly to him: lots of

smutty and inaccurate information about reproduction ensued amongst us boys.

Our Geography teacher, John Allidyce (call me 'John') was young, handsome and had just returned from an exchange year in the USA. He used to arrive in school in a battered Mustang, driven by his beautiful blond wife. He had us schoolboys spellbound by his description of life over there. You could, without too much effort, brighten up a lesson on coal output in the Northern Ukraine by getting him to talk about his experiences. 'And when I got to customs, I said "Good morning, How do you do? I am a teacher from England, come to teach in your country. Please do inspect my bags"'. Apparently, he was asked to repeat this a number of times as the officials were transfixed by his 'royal' accent, and caused quite a queue. Another time, he had us laughing with a story about going into a 'diner' and asking for a plain bacon sandwich. 'Bacon sandwich with lettuce and tomato – skip the mayo.' 'No, skip everything but the bacon'. Incredulity built up in the waitress. 'No lettuce or tomatos? I don't know if we can do that'. How exotic it all seemed to Kings Lynn schoolboys.

Mr Benson, our young Biology teacher, was entertaining and funny. He would often ask a boy in class how to spell 'futuristic', or 'inevitable' or even 'basically' when he was writing on the board. That was fine because, as he informed us at the beginning of term' I'm your bl—dy Biology teacher – I'm not expected to know how to spell!' We accepted the situation because we liked his honesty. He could lose his temper quite easily. Once, I remember, he was cheeked by a boy who was reported to be the son of an Indian Raja. 'Don't bl—dy well think you are someone because your father's a sodding king or something – get it?' He got it.

One or two were not so good. Our French master seemed to work on the principle of 'let's see how much we can embarrass the little runts'. To our terror, we would be made to stand up and reply to his questions in French. I can recall exactly the sweat and fear that this caused in me when I was 13 and 14. My distress at the thought of learning a foreign tongue only left me when I realized that what he was doing had no place in a school. This was a few years later when I myself trained to be a teacher: learning should always be a happy experience.

There was one master of old who used to fascinate us. He was apparently a very learned man who was Assistant Master at Lynn Grammar School and who

The under 15 football team at King Edward VII Grammar School, 1965. I am the one with the particularly gormless expression, back row, second left. I was big but otherwise not really gifted at the sport. I played at centre-forward at a time when every team played a five, three, two, one formation – none of the current four, four, two ones or one, three, four, two, ones etc. My biggest glory day was unfortunately not seen by many as it was foggy. In an inter-house match I scored 6 as we won 7-0 but practically no-one saw it, although the result stood.

I have always wanted to open the batting for England at cricket but a combination of having to wear glasses from the age of 14 – something to do with sprouting up so quickly – and a naturally jerky physical style meant I was not even in the school's reserve team. I think I had a vision of the game formed by the Hornung's Raffles novels where Raffles would languidly score a hundred and then spend the afternoons drinking Pimms on the pavilion balcony, the whole while being admired by all and sundry. As it was, my 'great' match was when I somehow managed to get 28 runs and also took a running catch in the outfield. It was so glorious.

I tried hockey once, against the local girls' grammar – they called them 'high' schools then. No fairer sex thing about it – they hacked your ankles to pieces. I gave it up.

Same with tennis: my racket seemed never to be at the same place as the ball.

My biggest glory day was in a sport I admire and love watching but have never really liked to take part in– Athletics. I was fifteen and the School Sports Day was upon us. We have remarked elsewhere in these pages that, since the mid nineteenth century, being 'academically challenged' (in current PC speak) has always been wiped out by greatness at sport. Well, we had a chap, Bing Courthould, who was big, athletic and, frankly, we sometimes wondered if his elevator went all the way to the top floor. BUT, he ruled the roost at the 100 metre hurdles, and, as such, had a pretty high status in the school. I was put against him in the hurdles. I had never run them before.

' So you're my latest sacrificial lamb, are you?', he said to me as we set our blocks.

'Yes, Bing' I replied, 'but I am sure I won't beat you'.

He just snorted. The race went off and, to my complete surprise, I beat him. He told me I was dead and all that kind of stuff, but he never recovered his previous status in school.

I got 'athletics colours' – a blue strip around my red blazer. You were also entitled, if you got 'colours', to have a huge and lovely badge on your pocket with the year of your triumph etched in gold . A few years ago, a friend of mine who is also a professor of Linguistics in Asia, wanted some pictures of an 'English schoolboy' to accompany his new book on the development of UK schools Could I help? I got the youngest of my friends that I could - and their kids, too - and photographed them in my blazer. The book has become a big hit in the Far East – reprinted several times as of this moment – and so my blazer and my victory over Bing Courthould lives on. I am not so sure, though, that he would be as chuffed about this as I am. I have my blazer still.

About blazers. Ours was a lovely deep red colour. If you could get 'colours' – that is, a band around it, blue for athletics (which is what I got), red for football, yellow for hockey and white for cricket – it looked spectacular. I always wanted blue and red 'cos it looked great intertwined. And the huge gold-enhanced badge, of course. The only boy who got all four in my time was Timpkins. Based on his sporting success, he got into Cambridge University. How I envied his blazer!

was also, alas, hanged for murder in 1759. His name was Eugene Aram and, to this day, debate continues as to whether or not he was guilty. Sir Edward Bulwer-Lytton wrote a famous novel about him in 1832 and he became a Victorian cause célèbre. He was accused of murdering one, Daniel Clark who may or may not have been having an affair with his wife, and with whom he was involved in a tawdry affair to do with stolen silver plate. In court he represented himself very eloquently, though evidently not eloquently enough, and many were the King Edward VII schoolboys who took up his cause in a reenactment of the complex case. The proceedings would generally peak with an emotional recitation of his last written words in the early hours of the morning that he was hanged (he tells us that it was after 3am because he had slept soundly until that hour):

> *Come, pleasing rest! eternal slumbers, fall!*
> *Seal mine, that once must seal the eyes of all.*
> *Calm and composed my soul her journey takes;*
> *No guilt that troubles, and no heart that aches.*
> *Adieu, thou sun! All bright, like her, arise!*
> *Adieu, fair friends, and all that's good and wise!*

My school has now been designated a Sports College. It admittedly has beautiful playing fields and, while I whole-heartedly support excellence in sport, I cannot but feel that Mr Small and all the staff who spent literally decades building up the place as a centre of academic excellence, and good old King Edward VII himself who took a genuine interest in the place, would have had great reservations.

Qualities needed for Primary Heads

One of the great things about the Halsgrove Community Histories is that they contain fascinating information about schooldays in our past which would have been otherwise lost – people's records and stories, and particularly photographs, perish with time. A great deal of this relates to primary education for the simple reason that, for many hundreds of years, nobody but the top echelons of society went to school beyond the age of 9 or 10.

We know what kind of person was wanted by communities throughout the land to head their schools. For example, the first record of a possible school in Sampford Courtenay, Devon in 1720 contains the following praise for …' *the proposed schoolmaster, Mr Thomas Cleary'… who is ' a person well skilled in reading, writing and arithematick and well able*

The rather austere features of Thomas Horlock Bastard (1796-1898), founder of the Blandford School, 20 miles to the north of Poole and Bournemouth on the South Coast.

and willing to instruct children and others as a schoolmaster, and the said Mr Cleary being a person of a sober life and conversation, and in all things conformable to the Church of England and for the encouraging of the pious education of poor children…' Not all were such beacons of light, though. Church records show that one, Humphrey Parish, received payment of £9 10s 10d for the schooling of six poor children in 1809-37 despite the fact that in 1795 he had fathered a ' base-born 'child of Mary Rapson in consequence of which he was charged with paying one shilling a week every week until the child was seven.

Again, early records show that some set questions for a bishop's visitation to a village such as Bridestowe in Devon included:

1. *Is any schoolmaster of good religion, sound teaching and licensed?*
2. *Does the schoolmaster receive communion and cause his pupils to do so?*
3. *Does the schoolmaster teach catechism?*
4. *Does the schoolmaster privately instruct in superstition, disobedience etc?*
5. *Are there any papists, and do they keep any schoolmasters?*
6. *Does the schoolmaster teach grammar other than the 'King's Grammar'?*

Above: *The schoolmaster of Mulbarton School, near Norwich, from January 1894 to September 1895, John Albert Vandyke, with his family.*

Left: *Ernest Gardner, seen here with his wife, was Headmaster of the County Council School, Markyate in the Chiltern Hills, from 1925-44.*

The County Council School in George Street, Markyate: it later became Markyate Primary School.

This 1910 photograph shows one of the first schools (left of the house on the corner) in Loddiswell, Devon, built about 1850,

This is a photograph taken in 1935 of St Ervan teacher, Dorothy Tippett, with her class of ragamuffins.

Group of teachers from the United Methodist annual Sunday-school treat, 1910, St Mawes Cornwall.

Headmaster John Tapp and Alice Yelland with class at the Church School, Lodiswell, South Hams, around 1900.

Staffing was very much a hit and miss affair, and assistant teachers could be incompetent. Inspections highlighted the problems. HM Inspector for Sampford Courtenay School concluded in a report dated 27.7.1894 that, regrettably ' *a high order of effi-ciency cannot be looked for with such a feeble staff.*' In 1898, the Inspector reported that ' *The school does not* make satisfactory progress.*' Nor could the powers-that-be remove the Headteacher, a Mr Challice, so it was with great relief that they were able to write in 1898 that ' *Challice, our very unsatisfactory schoolmas-ter, has beyond all our hopes got another appointment and resigned his post here. So now we hope for brighter things.*'

The British School, Loddiswell, South Hams, was built in 1853. This is the headmaster's house pictured in 1927: the size reflects his status in the local community.

Schoolchildren stand in front of The British School, New Road, Loddiswell, in 1907.

As a girl...

...and as a much loved teacher at Thorley Village School, near Bishop's Stortford, this is Gladys May Eagling: she is 21 here and is pictured in 1923.

Pupil teachers

The schoolmaster was often 'helped' by a pupil teacher: all well and good, sometimes, but hardly a recipe for guaranteed good teaching. *The Book of Sampford Courtenay with Honeychurch* tells us the following:

'Pupil-teachers were teenagers, usually former pupils, who were indentured for four or five years, receiving one and a half hours' daily instruction from the headmaster in addition to giving their own teaching. They worked at the same time for their annual examinations and for the Queen's Scholarship, the passing of which would earn them a place at training college. Some of the daily instruction at Sampford Courtenay was given during the lunch break. William Avery, aged 14 and son of George Avery, the Sampford Courtenay tailor, was taken on in 1877 and left in 1883, eventually progressing to an appointment as head teacher at Sticklepath Board School from 1889 to 1893. Charles Page, the 15 year old youngest son of Richard Page of Great Cliston, was the next pupil-teacher. He did not do so well. In fact 1887 HM Inspector commented: 'Charles Page has passed so bad an examination that my Lords have been unable to consider him as part of the school staff for the past year.'

Page nevertheless struggled on until early 1889, when Frank Richards, the 13 year old son of Thomas Richards, a railway labourer, took his place, initially starting as a monitor because of his young age. Richards did well and in 1894 he was helping with the upper classes. He took and passed the Queen's Scholarship and 'was presented with a leather travelling writing case subscribed for by teachers and scholars when he left the service of the Board in June 1894. Richards went on to Exeter Training College and, from 1898 until 1939, was the well-loved and respected headmaster of Sticklepath School.'

Women take up the profession

1921 marked a turning point in primary education as female heads and assistants became the norm. Subsequently, frequent changes in staffing interfered with the continuity of a child's schooldays. There was not the professionalism associated with the teaching profession that there is today and many a pupil must have become fond of, and accustomed to, a particular teacher only to find her replaced for the new term or year. The following details from the log of a west country school illustrate the state of play. In 1921 the

Above: *Carhampton First School, Somerset, celebrated its centenary in 1972. Here are some of the children plus, standing from left: Miss B Street (headmistress), Mrs Driscoll (teacher), Mrs Jean Webber (Governor) and Mrs Hutchinson (teacher).* Below: *Mrs Cook, the oldest living former pupil, is presented with a posy by Barry Webber, one of the youngest.*

The staff of Sir Walter Trevelyan School, Seaton, around 1922.

The Elementary School at East Lulworth, Dorset which was built in 1840 – this picture is from 1904.

Elmsett School, Suffolk 1897/8 with teachers, Miss Kells (back left) and Miss Young (back right).

The same school in 1950 with Miss Hollis sitting at the back.

Haughley Crawford's VC primary School, 1910. Haughley lies at the head of the Gipping Valley in Suffolk.

Inside Haughley Crawford's School c.1959.

Revd Burnaby wrote : 'Visited the school…. And found Mrs Gridgeman in charge and a kind of peace almost indescribable, and all at hard work and interested.' By April 1921, Ellie Hill was Headmistress, briefly assisted by her sister, Grace. In 1925 Agnes Lethem took over. Doris Horn, daughter of Bert Horn, the blacksmith, was appointed monitoress in 1922 and became an assistant teacher in 1925 (at a salary of £35 per year). She left to be married in 1926 and was replaced by Marjorie Kelland, who became Headteacher in 1932, assisted by Mary Skinner. Miss Kelland taught piano in the lunch hour and Myrtle Hunkin (née Hawking) remembers paying 6d for 20 minutes' tuition. Mary Bolt, as monitoress, covered Mary Skinner's absence on several occasions between 1931 and 1934. Mary Skinner left in 1934 to teach at another school. Ivy Reddaway was monitoress from 1934 to 1936. Mary Kelland left to marry Harold Cornelius, the bootmaker, in 1936 and Gladys Mounsdon became Headmistress, assisted by Evelyn Ball who in turn, was replaced by Mollie Clarke in 1938. In 1940 two new ladies were appointed as Headteacher and assistant. And so we could go on – the school logs up and down the land are very similar.

A few characters

People love recording their schoolday experiences and often these give a real 'feel' for days (just) gone by. They also remind us that some teachers and heads were real 'characters'. In *The Book of Looe*, Rebecca Whale tells us about her days in the local school, which began in 1943. The Headmistress at that time was a Miss Sloggett – a name to conjure with – who wore knitted suits. The school had what appeared to a five year old as a huge rocking horse, about twice her height. On the first day at school the class were told that if they were good during the day they would have a ride on the rocking horse before they went home in the afternoon. Rebecca was so afraid of it that when the time came for the first child to be lifted onto it, she started crying. The teacher smacked the child, thinking her tears were because she had not been first on. Rebecca had to go last, and it finally became apparent why she had been crying.

Another never-to-be-forgotten teacher was Miss George. Let *The Book of Looe* take up the story:

'Miss George took the 11-plus class, Rebecca being in a group nicknamed by the teacher 'the dumb five' because she scared the living daylights out of them and they were too afraid to answer questions. She would arrive at school wearing a Robin Hood style hat with a feather on the side, a hat she was proud of. When the class were at their 11 plus exam, Miss George retorted that if any of the 'dumb five' passed, she would eat her hat. When the results were read out and all five had passed, one girl stood up and asked if Miss George would be eating her hat. Not surprisingly, she was severely reprimanded!'

The schoolmaster was a man of considerable prestige in a community in Victorian times. Here, he is photographed with the other important citizens of Seaton in Devon. Left to right, back row: Harry Abbott, Harry Jones (the postman), CJ Gosney (the chemist), JG Oldridge , (the schoolmaster), Mr Strickland (bank manager), Samuel Good (the photographer), R Follett (the storekeeper), W Badcock (the carter). Front, Parson Beale, Doctor Evans, Parson Richardson.

Reading a story with Miss Phyllis Bailey at the Old School, Easton, near Norwich, 1950s.

Outside the Old School, Easton, in the late 1800s: the teacher is thought to be Mrs Sharp.

Inside the Old School, Easton in the big room, 1954: the teachers are Miss Bailey (left) and Mrs Pointer (right).

Headmaster, Mr W.H. Jones, with his charges at Manaton School on the edge of Dartmoor, 1913. As is often the case when children walked a long way to school, there is no disguising the muddy state of their hobnail boots.

Two teachers at the Old School, Easton, Norwich – left, Miss Taylor and right, Miss Bailey, in 1933.

'In one of the old classrooms a tall art cupboard stood in front of a long window, which opened at the bottom. The cupboard had no back, and by climbing into it the children could escape through the window into the alley at the back of the school, which led to the toilets. When Miss George was away for a few days, the unsuspecting new teacher turned around one afternoon to find half of the class had mysteriously disappeared.'

I wonder if C.S. Lewis had a similar cupboard in his schoolroom which inspired him to write *The Lion the Witch and the Wardrobe*?

A very good teacher, Mr Roberts, is described as follows in *The Book of Addiscombe, Volume II*, by Canning and Clyde Residents Association:

Mr Roberts was a very good teacher. He got the balance between education and learning just right. At a time when the process of learning was much more formal than it is now his approach was quite flexible. We were divided into groups according to our ability and the tables at which we sat were arranged in blocks facing each other. To a certain extent, at times when we were working on our own, as opposed to being taught from the front of the class, this meant that it was possible for all children to progress at the speed appropriate to the individual. Although it was only a beginning, we also learnt to count to about 44 in French

When I first read this, I was appalled at the cruel way Miss George acted but then I wondered if, perhaps, it was an act of genius to get the best out of her charges!

Not that the children were angels, but had a healthy love of fun, as the following little story tells us:

As remarked in the text, churches played a major role in the setting up and running of schools. The village school at Withycombe on Exmoor was built on land belonging to the glebe and there was a gate leading directly into the Rectory grounds. Here, the Revd Govan himself makes an appearance in a class photograph taken around 1904. Mrs F. Smith is the teacher.

Maria Purnell, Staverton School infant teacher, at the turn of the twentieth century. Staverton is in West Wiltshire.

Headmistress of West Coker School, Somerset, Miss Lillian Pooley and pupil 1920s.

This is Miss Pooley's class – she is seated in the middle.

The same school about twenty years earlier.

Miss Ivy Allen, a West Coker schoolmistress in the 1920s.

Mr Baldry, pictured here with Marjorie, was Schoolmaster of Northlew and Ashbury Parochial School, Devon , from 1900 to 1915.

– the reason for this number was that it was the number of children in the class and we all answered to our names with a French number each time the register was called.

Some headteachers were daunting, and some not. In *The Book of Honiton* by Gerald Gosling, we hear from Pearl Marshall (nee Mitchell) and her sister, Joan, who started school in the mid 1920s. Joan remembers that her first teacher was Miss Labdon and the Headmistress was Miss Wise. They liked Miss Wise as she would let the children stand around the heater in winter to warm themselves. She would also let Eddie Nichols bring a tray of freshly cooked warm buns from the Co-op and sell them to the children through the school railings for a half-penny each! In these days of practically universal central heating it is hard to imagine how cold life could be – Pearl and Joan's house in Exeter Road had no inside toilet or electricity. Bath night was once a week in a tin bath in front of the fire. There was no heating in the bedrooms but they sometimes warmed their bed with a hot brick. They would try to keep well fed by earning any extra pennies they could – for example, they picked wild primroses and violets which they sold to the local flower dealer who was called Joe Dyer. These would end up going by train to Covent Garden in London where they would be sold for far more than the 1d a bunch which the girls got for them.

The terror of Inspections

The fate of headteachers, assistants, pupil-teachers and monitors alike was decided by the Inspectors.

Pupils of Mulbarton School, near Norwich, on the Common after school in 1938. Describing the school dress at this time, Tony Kent wrote: 'Boys wore shorts to school and hobnail boots. Girls wore gymslips and knickers that covered all from navel to top of knee. Thick elastic held them in position. As the legs had elastic to hold them down, girls carried hankies, coins and sweets there. These knickers were known as 'Harvest Festivals' – 'all safely gathered in!'

Sculthorpe School, near Fakenham in north Norfolk, around 1909. The headmaster, Mr William Fawcett, stands on the left.

A school class in Bourton-on-the-Hill School in the Cotswolds in the 1960s, with the headteacher, Mrs Marjorie Buck.

HM Inspectors were virtually unchallengeable and still are. Jumping forward a little, I well remember the occasion of my own first inspection in 1976, when my innards turned to jelly as a well fed and satisfied looking man took his seat at the back of my class, which happened to consist of work-experience lads aged 17–25. We had had our run-ins as my predecessor as their English teacher had been a very beautiful blond lady and they were initially determined to do no work for me at all. So the rather risky strategy I adopted was making them sit in silence for three weeks and only communicate by writing – and writing for these lads was anathema. On the fourth week, we mutually understood that a truce was essential and we had a great time acting out job interviews in front of a video camera. I had grudgingly got their respect and once this is given, they will do virtually anything for you. So, here we were with an inspector in the class and the teacher in a sweaty funk. My throat was dry and no words would come. We were meant to be having a discussion class about business and the environment. After what seemed like an age, Jimmy Cheo, a building worker in a large firm in the town, cleared his throat: 'Well, sir (*Sir?* That was a first), is environmental pollution not caused by many different factors, as you were explaining last week?'

'Yes', echoed Brian Howard, an electrician, 'I found what you were saying very interesting'.

'I told my Nan when I got home and the family talked about it over tea'. This was Chris Hollins, a carpenter. Hands shot up all over the place after that as one chap after another said how much they enjoyed my classes.

I was off the hook and, if it is possible for someone to collectively fall in love with a class, I did it then.

Back at the beginning of the 20th century the Inspector had a more hands-on role and would test the children's knowledge. Until his retirement in 1899 Sampford Courtenay's inspector was Henry Codd, 'a tall, frock-coated, top-hatted, saturnine figure' who had the habit of rapping on school windows from horseback to announce his arrival. One member of the school, Richard Pyke, wrote the following:

'We were examined in this book (Goldsmith's Deserted Village*) by a pompous inspector. He asked what was meant by 'And every pang that folly pays to pride.' One of us got full marks by illustrating this profound observation by a reference to tight corsets.'*

Sometimes, there was open warfare between Inspectors and Heads. South Tawton and Soul Zeal with Sticklepath by Roy and Ursula Radford spotlights the 1928 Inspection of Sticklepath School:

Head's (Mr Richards) log, 22 May: School visited by Board of Education Inspector this morning. He arrived during playtime and immediately accused the Head Teacher of placing scouts on watch for his approach. He bases that accusation on the fact that he saw a girl run into school and tell the teachers that the Inspector had arrived. The master replied to his insulting remarks in no uncertain manner and it appeared to him that afterwards the Inspector went out of his way to ask questions in Mental Arithmetic too involved for any to follow and questions in Geography were purposely meant to confuse. This entry is made merely to explain beforehand any vindictive remarks that may appear on the report.

I don't want to go to school

There is a joke which goes as follows:

'Johnny, Johnny, get out of bed. It is time to go to school!'

'But I don't want to go to school, Mum!'

'Why not, Johnny?

'Because I am sick of it!'

'But, Johnny, you ARE the Headmaster!'

Time out of school was something that all schools had to deal with, and it was still very much a problem up until the 1950s and 1960s. Maurice Hutchins, former lifeboat coxswain, remembers his Cornish school in the 1940s:

'When I got old enough – I think it was from 11 or 12 years on – you could have a fortnight off school in the potato season. This was just after the war. I used to have my fortnight off, go back to school for a week and ask the headmaster for more time off as you had to have a ticket signed by him. I would get him to one side and say 'Mr West, you know my circumstances, I need the money. It's the only chance I've got to earn this extra money. And it was something like 2s9d for the man and 1s9d for the women. And of course, the boys, the children, they had the 1s9d.'

One of the great joys about researching a book like this one is that it gives you the perfect excuse to hang

The tradition of children helping with the harvest goes back several hundred years. This is a beautiful scene overlooking Veryan Bay, Cornwall, in 1953.

This was also taken in Veryan c.1920 – the whole family is joining in.

The National School, Mere, Wiltshire: these are children who have made unbroken attendances at school in 1898 – medals, flags and lots of fuss in an attempt to stop pupils absconding.

Another effort to reward good attendance – the 'Never Absent' photograph at the Board School, Markyate in the Chiltern Hills.

You could also get a fine certificate like this if you attended school regularly.

around second-hand bookshops and charity shops. In one, the Oxfam shop in Norwich, I found a bound edition of *Chamber's Journal of Popular Literature, Science and Arts* for 1887, containing dozens of pieces on aspects of late Victorian life. The following, although dated March 12 1887, is so typical of the problems encountered by schools regarding absenteeism until almost modern times, that I quote it nearly in full. Please bear in mind that some Victorian writers never let clarity of expression get in the way of 'big' words, preferably a few strung together, which they supposed demonstrated their erudition.

'Tales out of School* – Chamber's Journal of Popular Literature, Science and Arts , *March 12 1887*

A teacher's troubles are legion… In the nature of things he must suffer for born dunces. They are inevitable; and therefore, like bad weather or other disagreeable contingencies, they must be tolerated. But the thoughtlessness of parents who keep their children from school with little or no reason is a different matter. When the teacher is paid out of the grant, they rob him of money as well as reputation. It is, of course, to his interest to keep a watchful eye on these defaulters. …They excuse themselves in the most extraordinary epistles, of which the following is a specimen: 'Please excuse May. She caught a cold through getting her feet wet, and I must get her another pair before she can come to school.' When Jessie Black returned after a long absence, she also bore a note from her mother. This lady, according to her own statement, had been laid up with 'information in the back', which necessitated the girl's presence in the home. The teacher, with the best intention… hoped Bessie would take the same disease in her head.

The wonderful diseases which afflict school children often take the teacher down, as in the following instance. Mary

Jim Parson's threshing machine at work in Padstow, Cornwall, 1920. Children would try to help out and earn of few pennies, often encouraged by their parents: surely, this was much more useful than going to school?

Keen stayed away frequently with neuralgia. On her appearance, after a few days' absence, the teacher greeted her with: 'What Maggie – neuralgia again?' 'No, Sir,' she rather indignantly replied: 'it was not new-ralger, but the old ralger, that never went away!'

…Lizzie White was away for a week, but one morning she entered school with her eyes swollen. When the teacher went to ascertain the cause of her trouble, she began crying and said: 'We have something in our house, sir.' 'Indeed, ' said the teacher drawing back to avoid infection. 'Are any of you laid up with it?' 'Yes, sir, my mother.' – 'Sorry to hear that. You must get home at once'. Lizzie was on the point of obeying when the teacher asked: 'Has the doctor been?''Yes,sir.' And what did he say it was?' 'Oh, it's a boy!'.

…The gamekeeper's son who excused himself, with a bold face, because he had been watching game, nearly escaped undetected. At certain seasons, the game molested farmers, and he was employed, along with his father, in protecting crops. Considering the time of year, the teacher was at a loss to understand what crop required the services of Angus. 'Are you sure you have been watching game?' he said. 'Quite sure of that'. The emphasis on 'that' aroused suspicion. 'What game?' he asked. Angus looked crestfallen and confounded in a moment. 'What game. Sir?' Somebody whispered 'marbles'; and Angus was obliged to admit the impeachment.

A boy whose parents had just come to live in the neighbourhood, arriving late one morning, was called up to give an account of himself. 'Where have you been until this time?' said the teacher severely. 'Please, sir, I had to call at my uncle's'. 'What, you young rascal, you have no uncle in this town…I have caught you in the lie, and I will thrash you within an inch of your life.' 'Please sir, it's not the uncle you mean,' replied the boy, wiping his eyes: 'it's the uncle I have in every town!' Need it be said he meant the pawnbroker?

Want of clothes is one of the most common excuses that parents give for keeping their children from school. A schoolmaster in a rural district received the following: 'You must excuse Nellie, for it's not her fault – it's the calf's. Her only dress was out drying, and the calf ate it. But I will get a new one out of the calf for it.
NB – Jeamie Carter has promised to buy him.'

The step-mother who sent her husband's children to school almost naked, and when remonstrated with, said she 'didn't see no good in education, what did naught for people's outsides,' belonged to a class that harass the teacher more than any other. To them, inward benefits and

possibilities go for nothing. A child attends school day after day, yet what is there to show? It is a sheer waste of time, they will inform the teacher. They regard him with contempt, and the School Board Officer with detestation. The whole system is a fraud, to their minds, with no ultimate object beyond the annoyance of poor people. The children themselves imbibe these views. When a matchboy was asked how he accounted for his absence, he replied, proudly: 'Business; and there is no fooling there!' He obviously participated in what is a too common idea – that anything would be more manly than attending school.

Health care or lack of it

Those of us who went to school between 1920 and 1980 have at least benefited from rudimentary health care. I went to school in the 50s and 60s and can remember the dread of the 'school medical inspection' which seemed to consist of a man smelling of stale tobacco shoving his hand down my underpants and saying 'Cough!' Dental check-ups were even worse, consisting of real pain. I remember, when I was about 12, that the check-up was carried out in a room off the school dining room: the dentist thought I was being stubborn in refusing to let him push some filling into a non-existent space in my mouth. I have been terrified of dentists ever since.

Cue Margaret Robson, a lady who I feel I know well from The Book of Honiton, a little prior to my time in 1931. 'I can remember that dentist pushing a box-shaped thing into my mouth', she writes, having walked the two miles to school in dread about what was to happen. 'I was furious. I was to hate his visits ever after and always screamed and shouted each time I had to queue with the other children outside the rear cloakroom'. She reports that she had all her teeth out at the age of 29. Apparently, in some remoter parts of our kingdom as late as the 1980s, it was considered the ultimate treat and 21st birthday present to have all your teeth out and false one fitted. Thereafter, there should be no dental pain. Of course, false teeth had to be reliable and easy to keep in your mouth. This was not the case in bygone days, as the following story about the Duke of Wellington illustrates – it dates from about 1830. He had apparently been at a dinner with some important dignatories and the false teeth of one of the guests shot out of his mouth into the wine goblet of a Dowager Duchess. The problem with these early false teeth, made of whalebone, was that they tended to be loose in the mouth. Some indeed, had been other people's: looters after the Battle of Waterloo in 1815 collected, and sold on, many collected from dead soldiers. There being no modern paste or glue to keep them in place, the manufacturers instead inserted a powerful spring which must have made it murder to keep your mouth shut. Regrettably, after a few drinks, accidents could happen.

Some folklore cures

Just imagine how schoolday ailments were treated prior to these times. *The Book of Bridestowe* gives us some examples. A young person suffering from a cystic tumour had to be touched – 'strook' – by a gifted person an odd number of times on a Tuesday. A famous practitioner was Mr Blatchford. He was a Christian and appears sincere. He could offer prayers for a variety of ailments. One, for a sprain, read:

'Our Lord Jesus Christ rode over a bridge. His horse lighted, and He lighted; he said, 'Marrow to marrow, and bone to bone, and sinew to sinew, and blood to blood, and skin to skin, and to the others in the name of the Father and of the Son, and of the Holy Ghost, I cast this sprain away. Amen. So be it.'

If your baby was suffering from 'white mouth', parents should search the neighbourhood of Bridestowe until they found a donkey of the female sex. The baby was passed three times under the belly of the animal.

To cure bad boils on his neck a lad was advised to go into a field where daisies were growing. He had to go down on his hands and knees and eat the daisies but not touch them with his hands. On the first day he was to eat three and on the next five no more that two. He was cured.

Whooping cough was common in the 17th and 18th centuries. To cure it, you had to take the child into a field where there were sheep for three days in succession, sitting in a spot from where the sheep had just risen.

Such stories remind us that health care in schools is relatively recent. It is also true that anything beyond the most basic education has only been regarded as desirable in recent times. As late as 1940 almost a third of children did not go on to any kind of secondary education.

Primary School in Looe in the 1930s

Rebecca Whale went to Liskeard Grammar School in the 1940s and, as such, would have been one of a very privileged minority indeed. Rebecca remembers her mother giving her a felt hat to wear rather than a beret as it was more ladylike. It apparently lasted no more than a week before being discarded out of the train window on her way to school. When she was adult, Rebecca returned to her first school in Looe as secretary, and wrote the following poem printed in *The Book of Looe*, which gives a flavour of how it felt to be a young girl, both in and out of school, at that time.

I Remember

I remember going to the old school at West Looe,
And my father, sister aunts and uncle went there, too;
My grandfather helped build it, when he was just a lad,
But now they've got a new school, much nicer, and I'm glad.

I remember the fishermen, unloading their catch,
Then salting fish and icing them, ready for dispatch.
Into box and barrel they packed them very tight.
Loaded them upon the train to travel through the night.

I remember when the railways lines went straight down the Quay,
So goods wagons could be loaded with the fish, you see.
Then the steam train pulled its load of passengers and freight
To Scotland, Wales and Ireland or London's Billingsgate.

I remember the steamers, at anchor in the bay,
Bringing folk from Plymouth, so they could spend the day.
Picking up more visitors, to take them out to sea,
Out around the Eddystone, or Fowey, and back for tea.

A camera-obscura allowed us all to view
The happenings along the beach and Sea Front, here in Looe.
With donkey rides and sports events, shrimping in a pool,
And swimming lessons on the beach for classes during school.

I remember when the Downs Estate was vegetable plots,
And the Sea Front car park was where folk stored their yachts.
Barbican was mostly fields for grazing horse and cow –
Not rows and rows of houses, the way that it is now.

Trenant Point was woodland, where the herons used to nest
And none of the big houses took in a paying guest.
Walking in the Fore street, we all knew one another,
What's more, we knew whole families – grandparents, cousin, brother.

I remember August Fair, down on East Looe Quay,
Where we would watch for hours, my group of friends and me.
The circus too, came often, set up at Barbican,
Clowns, animals and jugglers, and gaily coloured van.

There were shops of ev'ry kind, in East Looe's crowded street,
Where you could purchase furniture, clothes or toys or meat.
There was no need to travel, by car or train or bus,
Everything you needed could be bought without a fuss.

I remember my grandad bought me 2d ice creams
And sweets bought for a penny, beyond your wildest dreams.
When fish and chips costs ninepence, and comics threepence each
And Punch and Judy shows were held, each weekend, on the beach.

Ah, yes, those were the good old days, when front doors were left ajar.
No crowded streets or beaches or noisy motor car.
But time moves on, and now we share our town with folk who visit.
It is not the peaceful place I used to know now, is it?

We leave our first boarding school under unusual circumstances

About a dozen years later I, like Rebecca, can remember the transition from primary to grammar school: it is a massive thing in a young person's life. Strangely enough, the exact date and nature of departure was determined by my sister.

My sister, Juliet, has always been up-to-the-minute as regards fashion. Ever since she was a nipper she has loved the colour, texture, feel and nuances of cloth. She was also, at the age of 16, a prime mover in hair-do's at the girls' boarding house she shared with her friends.

There was a thing then, amongst fashionable girls, for the 'beehive'. Us boys thought it very funny – a sort of blown up, back-combed hair arrangement which looked like a kind of airy football on otherwise pretty girls' heads. The head didn't like it and most girls would come to assembly in the local church at the beginning of the school day in a most decorous 1960s fashion – ie modest and lank.

Not so, my sister. One memorable morning, after hymns, the Reverend Quantock, addressed us all. His theme was 'morality'. 'And you will see,' he concluded, 'what will become of people who flout God's will.' He looked at Juliet. 'They become… they become… BAD'.

My sister was quickly up, tears welling up in her

eyes, and, young legs trembling, started to walk up the aisle of the church towards the exit.

'Come back here, now, Juliet Browning. You will report to my study after assembly'.

'No I will not', she replied.

'You are a disgrace to the good name of the school!' yelled the vicar.

'Don't care. I am leaving', said my sister and vanished, in tears and consternation, out of the West Door.

Now, the bravest thing about all this is that Juliet was convinced that our Mum would return her to the school for punishment. Reverend Quantock and our Mum had, up to this time, had a happy relationship. But when she reported these events to our Mum, all turned out quite differently. Mum was quick to confront the Revd.

'How dare you try to humiliate my daughter, like that?', she demanded.

The Revd said, ' how could you let your daughter come to school looking like that? Call yourself a Mother?'

Mum replied: 'Call yourself a priest?' and aimed a right-footed clump at his calf. She wasn't quite sure where to aim for 'cos he had a black cassock on but he cried out and limped, which was very satisfying.

'My daughter and both sons are leaving – right now'. I was about 11 and a half and my bro' a couple of years older. And that is how my brother and I ended up in grammar school. Juliet had had enough of schools.

Chapter Eight

A Chapter of Schoolday Memories – Part Two

school, friendships, family, special days, punishments and games

*Soap and education are not as sudden as a massacre,
but they are more deadly in the long run.*
MARK TWAIN

O! this learning, what a thing it is.
The Taming of the Shrew,
WILLIAM SHAKESPEARE

Here are some more schoolday memories.

Sweets on the way home 1930s
From *The Book of Blofield and Hemblington*
Barbara Pilch

Roy Jermy's first teacher in the infants' class was Miss Dolly Bailey:

She was a kind lady with a lot of patience. She lived with her mother, who kept a general shop not far from the school. We used to call in on the way home at her mother's shop, when we had sufficient money, to buy a few sweets. She used to have rows of tall jars of various sweets of different colours and flavours.

I remember at the end of each school day in the infant class we used to sing 'Now the day is over, night is drawing nigh, shadows of the evening steal across the sky', and we used to sing it with such gusto as we knew it was the end of the day and we would be on our way home.

After school and meeting boys
From *The Book of Fareham*
by Lesley Burton and Brian Musselwhite

Pam Webb is talking:

My most enduring memory is of being met by my mother outside my school, which was Wykeham House, in the High Street and being taken to the cinema. As school

finished at 3.30 pm, there was plenty of time to visit the café at the Savoy Cinema before seeing the film. Decorated in Art Deco style and with french-windows and a balcony, I thought it was wonderfully 'grown-up'. Because of the time, we always saw the 'big' picture first, and if we didn't like the 'second' picture we just left and went home. Once there was a practice air-raid and tear gas was used and we had to sit and watch the film wearing our gas masks. Being right opposite the bus station it wasn't far to go for the bus. Sometimes we went to the Embassy, which wasn't quite as exciting as there was no café.

I expect everyone remembers that lovely shop Letherens and the overhead rail network that ran to the cashier's office. Absolutely fascinating, watching the little wooden pots whizzing along the wires and then returning with the change. A more upmarket shop was Philip's, where they sold, amongst other things, very posh hats. Woolworth's was a good mecca to head for. If you were lucky, you might just catch a consignment of pencils, rubbers and note-books, all of which were in short supply in the war years. Later on, when we were a little older, the L-shape of Woolworth's was useful to meet the boys from Price's School, amongst gardening tools and household items and out of view of the rest of the shop.

Another interesting place was Pyle's, a cake shop and restaurant. Very occasionally, I had lunch there as a change from school dinners. The shop always smelled of sweet cakes and icing sugar. We were on our honour to go straight back to school after having lunch, but some of the more daring girls stayed out and met the boys from Price's.

Cornwall's Rumford Village in 1895. Behind such picturesque scenes was often great hardship.

Christmas performance
From *The Book of Sculthorpe* by Gary Windeler

The Dereham and Fakenham Times wrote the following regarding a performance by the children 24 December 1891:

The children of the National School gave a cantata on Christmas Eve called A Bundle of Sticks. The stage was tastefully arranged as a room with a Christmas tree in the middle, while a funny old elf, Santa Claus by name, came with his sack full of presents for the children. The parts were nicely acted, the singing both of solos and choruses being of superior merit. The master (Mr Hedgethorne) deserves much credit for having trained the children so well. Mrs Hedgthorne accompanied on the piano, which she kindly lent for the occasion. Sir Lawrence and Lady Jones and family were present besides a fair number of parents. Christmas carols concluded a pleasant evening.

War time bravery 1917
Mr Fawcett's entry in the school log book for Friday 9 March 1917 was as follows:

At the close of school today the children assembled in the main room, and there were also present the rector and Mrs Labouchere and several parishioners. The occasion was the

Blandford Carnival, Dorset 1892.

Blandford Carnival 1960s – Jean Tattersall and family go a milking.

presentation of a certificate awarded to Edna Rutland (13) by the Royal Humane Society for conspicuous bravery on January 30th in saving the life of a school fellow, Mabel Lusher, from drowning. Several children were sliding on a pond on the Glebe just before morning school and Mabel Lusher ventured on a dangerous part near the middle of the pond. The ice broke and the child fell into very deep water. She would have drowned but for the presence of mind of Edna who very bravely crawled to the edge of the bending ice and rescued her. The Reverend JA Labouchere recounted the circumstances and also gave a brief history of the RHS after which Mrs Labouchere handed the certificate to Edna, and the children gave hearty cheers for their brave schoolfellow.

The Punishment book

From *The Book of Easton*
Easton Village History Project

Punishment book of St Peter's School

DATE	NAME	AGE	OFFENCE	PUNISHMENT
4.10.1926	Arthur	11	Insolence	2 strokes of cane
10.7.1930	Gerald…	8	Rubbed hole in book and told untruth about it	2 strokes on hand
14.4.1931	Basil…	10	Stoning a beggar singing near school	4 strokes on hand
6.10.1931	Dick…	12	Cracking a nut in school	3 strokes on hand
25.11.31	Thomas…	8 and half	Said he didn't care after coming in late	1 stroke on hand
25.11.1931	Charles	8 and half	Catching and kissing and otherwise annoying 8 girls	slaps on buttocks
21.1.1932	Gerald/Gordon		Treating girls disrespectfully	2 strokes each with stick
3.3.1932	Gerald	10	Cheating sums	2 strokes of stick
17.7.1933	Tom	10	Putting pencil up nostril and untruthfulness about it	2 strokes with stick
10.9.1942	Lawrence		Tore a double page from his Scripture book and stuffed it in the hedge	1 stroke on each hand

Six naughty boys from Watchet in Somerset caught on camera smoking on the West Street beach, around 1925.

All aboard the charabanc for the West Coker village outing! Hats and caps were almost universal in the 1920s.

The Empire Educational Series.

Department

School

SCHOOL PUNISHMENT BOOK,

DESIGNED TO MEET THE REQUIREMENTS OF

Educational Department Revised Instructions

(APPENDIX II., SEC. 32).

JARROLD & SONS,

EDUCATIONAL PUBLISHERS,

10 & 11, WARWICK LANE, LONDON, E.C.

PRICE ONE SHILLING.

VE Party in Beckenham.

This is David A Berwick again:

The Crome Secondary Modern School 1958 & 1959

This fine little school, (sadly gone) was situated on Telegraph Lane in Thorpe Hamlet, Norwich and I did well there. I was keen on English, geography, religious education, music and history. I also developed into a good athlete. All in all, I was very happy at that school and again, it all came down to some really nice teachers. Mr Bellchambers, (had the nick-name 'ding-dong') was head when I arrived there and he also sometimes taught history. Mr Murray, (English), Mr Softley, (geography), Mr Atkinson, (music), Mr Chivers, (RE), Mr Fenwick, (history), Mr Drane, (metal work) and Mr Towler, (wood work) were my pick as the best from my point of view. As a matter of interest, I have to this day always remembered and put into practice Mr Drane's advice when cutting anything. "Always make sure you have both hands behind the cutting edge boys". Mr Chivers could be a bit fearsome I recall if you crossed him. For instance, he disliked anyone using a fountain pen. You had to use the old-fashioned dip pen and use the ink well provided. A number of us craftily got around this by filling our fountain pens with school black ink, then, holding the pen tightly next to the horrid dip-pen, at a distance, he never noticed that we were, in fact, using our fountain pens! If he did venture from his front desk and wander down my row, I would quickly make the fountain pen disappear, and he would be none the wiser!

"Where's the slipper gone?"

During these times it was still quite usual for miscreants to 'get the slipper' on the backside if warranted. There was a piano in the library as well as the main hall and the music room. We sometimes had lessons in the library, mostly music I recall. The dreaded slipper was actually left hidden in the top of the piano, and, when needed, the teacher would go to the instrument and throw up the lid and out would come the slipper! It would be brandished at the poor culprit due to receive it followed shortly afterwards with it smacking on the rear end of said boy. Totally out of character one day before the teacher arrived in the room, I decided to hide the slipper elsewhere, much to everyone's delight. Come the inevitable moment of its need, the piano lid was thrown up as usual, a hand went inside to collect said item only to be immediately withdrawn in annoyance at not finding it. "Who has moved the slipper?" was the withering call. Absolute silence reigned, nobody broke ranks. "Right, you'll all miss break for this" was the response. Feeling guilty that my mates would all be punished I owned up, and gave him the hidden slipper.

"Berwick, I don't believe it! You've never given me cause to punish you have you?" "No sir". "Have you ever had the slipper?" "No sir" You realise I'll have to punish you?" "Yes sir" "Right, get over here and bend over this desk. You realise this is going to hurt?" "Yes sir" Thwack! Thwack! The room resounded. My god it did hurt. I thought afterwards whilst looking through wet eyes, that he might have been a little more lenient for a first, and only, offence. A bit of a good jape had cost me dearly. It was the worst moment for me at that school which was otherwise a fine place to be educated at.

Outward Bound Miracle

In January 1959 the new Head, Mr Killingbeck, (known as 'Killer') called me to his office to tell me that I had been selected, with one other Norwich boy, to go to the Duke of Edinburgh's Outward Bound Centre at Ullswater in the Lake District, for one month. At age 14 I was the youngest on the course, and it was very, very tough. One amazing thing happened there one Sunday. I had been spud-bashing in the kitchen and was quite keen to get away to go to church. I had been brought up that way, was missing home and I felt it would be comforting to go. Eventually, I got away about 10:20am and then dashed off to cover 4 miles to the nearest church at a charming village called Watermillock, where the service started at 11am. What with the hilly terrain I was not going to make it on time. I kept going. Suddenly I was aware that an almost silent-running large car was coasting to a halt beside me. It must have been a Daimler or Bentley. Really posh. A charming lady spoke from the window and asked if I was going to the church. Suddenly believing in miracles I gasped yes! "In

Lunch break at Bakewell Cubs' training day, April 1969.

you get young man", she said. As the vehicle smoothly glided up the hill this sweet lady turned to me and asked me where I was from. I said Ullswater. She then enquired where in England did I come from. I said Norwich. She turned to her husband who was driving and said, "Did you hear that darling, this young man comes from Norwich". His reply was something like, "Well bless me, really?" Now here's the tasty bit. She turns back to me and says, "My husband, Mr Pierce, designed your City Hall, and met the King there in 1938". I was rather overcome with it all and doubt I made a fully appropriate response. What an utterly amazing thing to happen to a breathless homesick kid from Norwich!

Friendships and play 1950s
From *The Book of Orchard and Eden Park*
by Ian Muir and Pat Manning
David Hepburn, Edenstone FC, remembers:

I was born in 1947 about a year after my parents moved into their newly constructed prefab in Eden Park Avenue. Originally designed to last about ten years, prefabs were a short-term solution to the postwar housing shortage. For the time they were modern, well equipped and comfortable, with a fully fitted kitchen including electric cooker, fridge and running hot water which, together with the modern bathroom with bath, basin and separate loo, made them

desirable homes, with rent and rates of 18s6d. I and my two brothers best remember the large garden backing onto Harvington playing-fields. In the early days I recall walking up to the rear fence to watch the cows grazing but within a few years the field was turned into a sports field with football in the winter and cricket in the summer.

I spent many long summers with the other boys from the road, in particular the Russells, Turneys and Lowes, playing football or cricket or building camps and climbing trees in the woods behind the fields – an absolute paradise for boys of our age. Those summers seemed to go on and on, and the community spirit and friendships formed then were to last a lifetime.

We regularly attended St John's Church, just a few minutes' walk away, and were members of the choir and the Campaigners. Under the choirmaster, Mr Brookman, we would sometimes attend the church three times on a Sunday and during the spring and summer would look forward to earning extra pocket money by singing at weddings on a Saturday.

The lads that used to meet at Harvington at that time represented the beginnings of what was later to become Edenstone Football Club. It is testimony to our outdoor upbringing that the club, at the time of writing, runs a

The cricket team of Sebright in the Chiltern Hills, early 1930s.

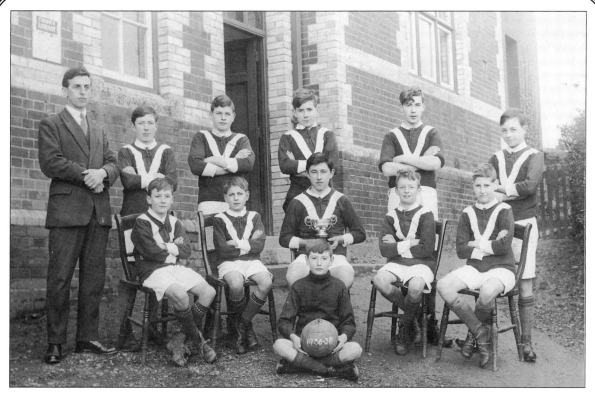

A great picture of the football team of St Mawes, Cornwall in 1930/31.

Heavy bombing raids constantly set off from the airfields of Norfolk during the Second World War and children learnt to tell the type of aircraft and whether or not it was friendly by the sound of the engines. The Roman Catholic Cathedral in Norwich, situated on the highest ground in the city, acted as a welcome beacon on their return. This is a USAAF Liberator flying over the Norfolk village of Hempnall.

team known as 'the Legends', which includes many of the prefab boys, now well into their fifties. The prefabs were demolished in around 1968/69, some 20 years after construction, but the friendships continue.

1926 Separation of boys and girls
From *The Book of Peter Tavy with Cudlipptown* by Peter Tavy Heritage Group

Although local and national education authorities increasingly imposed their rules on building standards and suitable accommodation for teaching, the extension now used as a kitchen was not built until 1926, when £106 was collected in the village to do the work and provide more space. The outside toilets were an early requirement. Betty Wilton (nee Leetoose) remembers the girls leaving by a door at the back of the hall, which looked out onto a grass play area, to reach their toilet, while the boys left by the front door, going across the hard playground to reach their toilet, which was back-to-back with the girls' and divided from them by a high wall. There was no flush system and just two buckets in each place. Similarly, when James Perkins was at school, during school break the girls played on the grass area that had flower beds and the boys played on the tarmac below.

Home is bombed
From *The Book of Fareham*
by Lesley Burton and Brian Musselwhite
Pam Webb recalls:

They (German bombers) also dropped their surplus bombs in the mud on the way home and in the morning there was often mud on the roads and roofs of the houses. Later in the war, Portchester had a very bad night! It must have been 1943 as I had just started my new school. Where the Seagull Public House is now, at Cornerway Lane, a bomb from the previous night's raids had exploded, leaving the largest hole I have ever seen; it was years before the hole was filled in. Several people were killed in the Crossways, and that particular night our back door blew off and the dining room windows were smashed in on top of the Morrison shelter. The gas was cut off and in the morning my mother turned our little electric fire onto its back and boiled the kettle on it to make a cup of tea. Lying in bed at night I could hear the trains on the railway line; sometimes the sound of the goods trains went on and on throughout the night. I now realize this must have been the build-up to D-Day

Long summer holidays

During the long hot summers when we were not making jam or bottling fruit, my mother and I used to walk. As the proper beaches were all out of bounds during the war, we made do with the creeks around Portchester Castle. I did all my paddling on the muddy flint and seaweed-covered beaches, always hoping to find a Roman coin, but never being successful. We often took my friend with us and our favourite walk was down Castle Street to Cow Lane and then across the water-meadows and what was left of the medieval malting. From there you could look northwards across the upper reaches of the harbour to Portsdown Hill, and westward to the backs of the long gardens of the very old houses and cottages in Castle Street. We came up through the Iron-Age ditch to the Castle, just by the Land Gate. If the weather was good and we didn't need the shelter of the castle walls, we went through the Water gate and turned right and walked round to the Urchins Meadow, usually full of cows, and sat under the sea wall. We had picnics of things like jam or chocolate spread sandwiches and my friend and I would share a bottle of Tizer lemonade, and my mother would usually have a flask of tea. Sometimes we went home on a different way along Wicor Path, so-called as it once led to Wicor Mill, by then long gone. On its site was a bone factory that made glue. The smell was dreadful and we always knew when it was going to rain as the west wind blew the smell across Portchester.

Cricket-mad teacher
From *The Book of South Stoke with Midford*, edited by Robert Parfitt
A pupil at the village school from 1930-35 remembers his teacher:

She wasn't strict at all, and we didn't learn all that much. She was mad about cricket, though, and used to play with us every break time. If we couldn't get her out by the end of break time, she'd sometimes keep us out in the playground till lunchtime, trying to bowl her out.

Boy terror
From *The Book of Crudwell* by Tony Pain

11 March 1936

E— aged 14 years caused some considerable trouble in the school today. The boy has caused considerable trouble ever since his admission., 19.9.32. His behaviour has been very insulting both in and out of school, one child's parents having to seek police protection from his abuse. 1.30 pm. When spoken to today for his behaviour in his lines he stood grinning most insolently and then shouted out and ran out of school. The Head Teacher is writing to the Managers as his conduct is most detrimental to the whole tone of the school. 1.45 pm. This boy returned to the school

Scouts at camp in Ashwell, Wiltshire, around 1915.

When the Revd T.S. Dawson married Miss Eileen Govan, daughter of the rector of Withycombe, Somerset, in 1931, Carhampton Scouts formed a guard of honour as well as pulling the wedding cart to the vicarage where this photograph was taken.

A lovely picture of a Sunday school outing in Markyate, Herts, during the Second World War.

evidently thoroughly ashamed of himself. After considerable bravado, he calmed down and apologized for his
unseemly behaviour. He has now been given a last chance.

Evacuee's school day
From *The Book of Thorley*.
Compiled by the People of the Parish
Mike Teitz is talking:

*Thorley School stood in a small playground, next to the
schoolmaster's house. It had a 'little room' for the infants
and a 'big room' for the older children. The big room was
lit at each end by lancet windows, which, with the high
ceiling, gave a slightly ecclesiastic air.*

*Mrs Smith was a rather formidable lady – at least to a six
year old boy. Every day, she bicycled a great distance from
the other side of Bishop's Stortford on a creaky, upright
machine. On arrival she would remove her high button
gaiters, with a button hook that made a loud popping noise.*

*We learned to write by copying from the blackboard on to
slates using thin slate pencils that made squeaky noises.
Another never-to-be-forgotten part of our day was fraying.
We were each handled a bundle of cloth scraps and shown
how to pick them apart to create a pile of fragments of
thread, which was then stuffed hard into cylindrical white
cloth tubes perhaps three inches in diameter, then sown up.*

*We were told that these would be used to support the limbs
of wounded soldiers in hospital.*

*In due course, we moved up to the big room with Miss
Moorhouse. This was a very different place – almost a
different century. Miss Moorhouse believed in learning 'by
doing', as well as a thorough grounding in reading,
writing and mathematics. And she did it all by herself in
one room with children ranging in age from seven to four-
teen years old.*

*With Miss Moorhouse we were never bored. Somehow, she
managed to teach us all the usual things, while also ensuring that something interesting was always happening or
about to happen. To teach reckoning and money, we
constructed a shop, using empty packages and tins from
home, creative signs, labels and prices, and buying and
selling with money that we designed and made. We sang
the old songs, accompanied by Mrs Smith on the piano. We
also danced country dances: I was in awe of the older boys'
sword dance with its circling and clashing of wooden
swords. At various times we acted out historical episodes,
creating costumes at home. One year I was David in the
story of David and Goliath.*

*Art was another part of our school experience. I don't know
how she found the materials in wartime, but Miss
Moorhouse always had us drawing, painting and model-*

ling. I think my love of art comes from this time. Miss Moorhouse's philosophy included creating a school garden, where we dug and planted, raised chickens, and tended a goat. Miss Moorhouse would take us to the pond in the neighbouring meadow to examine newts and collect tadpoles, where we would slosh about and collect frog-spawn, hoping for it to turn into frogs.

We also learned to swim, taught by Miss Beryl Frere, who lived with her sister in the grandest house in the village, Twyford House. Beginners were placed in a canvas loop attached to a rope. Miss Frere would walk back and forth on a narrow bridge across the stream supporting the flailing would-be swimmer, calling out encouragement and instructions for the breast stroke. Those who succeeded then moved to the millpond.

Thorley School gave me a wonderful education up to the age of ten.

The Diamond Jubilee

On 24 June 1897, 13 year old St Mawes schoolgirl, Ellen German wrote the following account:

As everyone knows on Tuesday it was the Jubilee. All over the British Empire the Diamond Jubilee was kept up. Sunday was the day of Victoria's accession but the celebration was not had until Tuesday. In London they had beautiful weather but I am going to tell you about the celebration in our parish. The children went down on the quay early, and about a quarter to two the medals were given away, all the children who were there had medals. After this we formed a procession and marched up the parade, the ministers went first, then came the band and after this the big and small boys, then the girls and behind the women. We went into JC Kennerlly Esq's ground and there sang a verse of the National Anthem. Then we came up around Castle Lane and went into the Jubilee field. When we got

YOU ARE ABOUT TO BECOME A SOLDIER. This will mean a big change in your life. You will find yourself performing unfamiliar duties in a new atmosphere.

At first, naturally, you will feel rather strange to your surroundings: you will miss your home and friends. But you will soon realise that your comrades are in the same position, and that you are all starting from the same mark.
Later, when you have grown more familiar with your duties, and the reasons at the back of these duties, you will realise something else—namely, the greatness of the service which you are to-day rendering to your country ; a service which that country will always gratefully remember.

Here are three words of advice :—

(1) Learn to obey all orders smartly and without question. This is not a mere matter of outward show : very often the lives of an entire body of men may depend upon the prompt action of a single individual. The more thoroughly you acquire that habit the safer you and those who serve with you will be, and the sooner we shall achieve final victory and peace.

(2) Acquaint yourself with the traditions of your particular corps or unit, and live up to them. This will lead you to take a pride in its history, and will foster in you the team-spirit, commonly known as *esprit de corps* which is the life-blood of the soldier.

(3) The British Army draws peculiar strength from the close relations which have always existed between officers and men. The officer's first duty is to his men : he not only leads them into action, but he is responsible for their welfare and comfort at other times. He joins in their games, he listens to their troubles. Therefore, whenever you stand in need of aid or advice, do not hesitate to approach him (through your serjeant or other non-commissioned officer) and tell him the whole story.

Once more I welcome you to the Army. Fear God, Honour the King, and May Victory Soon Crown Our Arms !

THE WAR OFFICE   *Secretary of State for War*

Many young men went straight from the classroom into the Forces. This letter from the War Office tells them what to expect.

An enchanting picture of happiness at (almost) the end of six years of war: VE Day party in Fareham, Hampshire, May 1945.

The children of the junior school at Wicor, Fareham celebrate the coronation of Queen Elizabeth II in 1953. Would the accession of the glamorous new Queen at last usher in a time of plenty? Regrettably, no.

Gwendoline Marsh and Elsie Howse 'take the waters' at Seaton, Devon in 1903.

George Martin, of Mulbarton six miles south of Norwich in Norfolk, won second prize with this decorated bicycle at the George VI Coronation celebrations, 1937.

in the sports began. I was not there to see the first two races but I was there to see the rest. At half past four the children had their tea, and a good tea I had. After this the grown up people had their tea, and the games continued until eight o'clock. About this time it was damp and foggy and many people went home for their jackets. Many young people stayed there and played two's and three's until 9 o'clock. About ten o'clock a big bonfire was lit and we had to keep a good way from it, we could see one at Pendennis Castle and several in other places. When I got home it was eleven o'clock and I was very tired. After having my supper I went to bed wishing we had a holiday again the next day.

Christmas 1919

Muriel Dotson, born 1906, recalls:

On Christmas Eve I usually go to Falmouth with my Mother or Father or sometimes with both. When I go I buy some presents for my friends. After I come home in the evening I go singing with my friends about half past six. When we have finished going to people's doors singing we share the money. Afterwards I go to my Grandmother's house with my Mother until about ten o'clock and then we go home. On Christmas day when I wake up I look into my stocking to see what is in it. After I dress I go downstairs and give my Mother and Father a present each and wish them a happy Christmas. When all that is over we have breakfast and then I clear the things away and we go to my Grandmother's house. On Boxing day in the morning I generally go to Sunday School where we decorate it for the bazaar, which we have in the afternoon….. In the evening there is usually entertainment and I am often in it.

Christmas time: 1920s and 1930s

Charlie Collins remembers:

Preparations for Christmas started during the summer, where eggs were pickled in large brown earthenware jars of isinglass. The eggs were then used in Christmas cakes. The cakes were made at the beginning of November and it was always a major operation. One of my tasks was to sit at the table and sift through the currants, raisins and sultanas, making sure all the pips were removed.

The cake mixing was done in a large earthenware bowl and we all had turn to take at stirring. The mixture was then placed in cake tins, the largest being about 10 inches in diameter.

The cakes, about two at a time, were placed in the oven of the coal stove. These were moments of great tension while the cakes were cooking, in case they did not rise. When they were deemed to be ready all the doors to the room were closed and were not allowed to be opened in case a draught made the cakes collapse. Then they were taken out and placed on the kitchen table to cool…

Christmas pudding making, like cakes, was again a major operation, with many being made several weeks before

The Carne Hill Chapel Band of Hope enjoying tea and giant saffron buns in 1911.

This is how you bought your Christmas meat early in the 20th Century – the turkey or goose would come complete and pigs could be bought by the half. It needed to be a cold winter because outside larders were where meats were kept.

Christmas. They were boiled in a large cast-iron container on the stove. The pudding mixture was placed in a white basin and covered by a white linen cloth, tied in a knot at the top. By this it was lifted out of the pot.

Ox tongue was another preparation for Christmas. It was boiled in a large cast-iron container on the stove. When cooked it was taken out and placed in a round press. The top was put on and screwed down, compressing the tongue. This was eaten at supper over the Christmas period.

Ham was also cooked and served for supper.

Pickling onions was also a part of the Christmas catalogue. This started at the end of August, when shallots were bought. During the evening they were peeled and put into large jars with vinegar and cloves.

In the garden was a Bramley apple tree, from which there was always a large crop of really big apples. These were picked and placed on shelves in the dark cupboard under the stairs. They were then used as required throughout the winter, usually with apple pie and cream. There was always a large apple pie for Christmas.

The turkey (we always had turkey) arrived from one of the local farms three or four days before Christmas. It was complete with head, feathers, insides and feet. The feathers had to be plucked, which was quite a long job, especially picking out the small ends of quills that remained. The turkey was then scorched with a lighted candle to burn off all the ends that remained. After cleaning and washing it was then placed in the outside safe until Christmas morning.

Auntie Sheba (Sawle) made a sponge for every Sunday tea (made with 'green' sponge mixture unknown today). For Christmas she made at least two…

Drinks such as beer, spirits and such were never around. There was usually a bottle of sherry received as a present, but this was put away in the cupboard and used sparingly over the next year.

We had plenty of mixed nuts placed on the table to help ourselves. Using the nutcracker when we were small restricted the amount we could eat.

There was very little drinking at all at homes over Christmas or at any other time. Uncle Harold Watts made sloe wine and Uncle Alf Pascoe … made several kinds of home-made wine. Men went to the four public houses, the Rising Sun, the Victory Inn, the Ship and Castle and the St Mawes Hotel, and over Christmas quite a lot of noise and singing came from there. Ladies did not go into public houses in those days.

Going to bed on Christmas Eve, I always hung my pillow-case at the bottom of the bed. The next day it contained oranges, apples, a coconut, sweets and maybe one toy, and when I was a little older mother's present was a dictionary or an atlas.

It was all hustle and bustle on Christmas morning, with Aunt Sheba, my mother and father and sister Sheba, with Douglas and myself sitting in the window seat.

Christmas tea was in the lower front room. During the afternoon Dain would arrive and he would play games with us. Tea was Christmas cake, tinned fruit, mince pies, tartlets and cream scones. We had cream with everything.

The coal fire was topped up with logs and the room was warm. In the evening we played games – Ludo, and Snakes and Ladders.

There were a few decorations put up in the front room. The main item was a real tree, and this was placed in a large container of earth. The glass decorations were similar to those we get now, but the lights were small candles placed in small tin candle holders to catch the grease. The candles had to be watched very carefully so that they did not catch the tree on fire.

Favourite household duties 1920
As recounted by Muriel Dotson on 2 February 1920

I like cooking the best of any work. Because for one thing it is very useful and for another it is a thing everybody should know. I often watch my Mother making dinners and cake. Sometimes if she has a little dough left over I make a jam pasty or if she has a little meat left make a potato and meat pasty. One day when my Mother was out I made a small pasty for my tea with some dough my Mother had left. It tasted very nice, but not as good as what my Mother makes.

Muriel Dotson's remarkable record
In 1918 the local newspaper reported the following attendance record:

A remarkable record has been set up by little Muriel Dotson, daughter of Mr and Mrs Joe Dotson, Grove Cottage. Aged 12 years, she has attended school for the past six and a half years, not once being either absent or late. On hearing of this creditable record, Sir George Smith awarded Muriel a bound volume of the Girls' Own Annual, and unable to be present through indisposition, he delegated Mr Spargo James to make the presentation,

which took place recently. Inside the front cover is inscribed: 'Presented to Muriel Dotson by Sir George Smith, chairman of the District Education Committee, in recognition of her six and a half years of punctual and unbroken attendance at St Mawes Council School'.

First day at school 1950
From *The Book of Shaugh Parish* by Don Balkwill

Shaugh Prior CP was my first school. It's not changed much in over 50 years except that it now has an extension and inside toilets, which it didn't have in my day. I started school on 7 September 1950. How can I be so precise? I've seen, and have a copy of, the original register. The school itself was built in 1881. The school was, and still is, very small. You walk through the entrance foyer into the corridor. It still has the children's coat hooks on the left hand wall. As you go down the corridor, the door on the right led into the infant classroom, and the door on the left to the junior classroom. The junior classroom doubled as the dining room because the kitchens are on the far side of this classroom. There was, and still is, a hatch in the far wall through which school dinners were served. The total number of children in the school varied between 30 and 50. I attended the school from 1950 to 1956. My first memory of the school is my very first day. My mother took me to the school and tried to leave me. I screamed and screamed, I suppose because I was scared. I had had no experience of interaction with other children at that stage. I was hanging on to my mother and pleading with her not to leave me. Of course she had to, and eventually I was dragged into class. Whether we were told then what the rules for going to the toilet were, or whether my mother had told me previously, I don't know. What I do know is that later in the morning I put my hand up to go to the toilet and was given permission. Instead of going to the toilets, which were outside, I proceeded to do a runner and went home. My mother, of course, took me back to school again. I don't know if I was punished for escaping, but I rather think not because I have no memory of it. I now have very fond memories of the two teachers there, Mrs Nelmes, the infant teacher, and Mrs Armistead, who taught juniors and was also the headmistress.

Games we played
From *The Book of Addiscombe, Volume II*, by Canning and Clyde Residents Association

The boys, on the whole, while waiting for school to commence, played with cigarette cards (swapping them), marbles of clay then glass – my father stated 'we' cheated as it was certainly not played like he used to – and the grand game of conkers. All games were played in their respective seasons governed by childish rules which,

Helping Dad - Bert Tidmarsh and son Bernie man the mobile forge in the Wiltshire village of Crudwell.

A charabanc outing for Blofield children, Norfolk, in 1925.

Beating the bounds in Lustleigh, Dartmoor in 1924, once a very important ritual.

This is the same ceremony at another Dartmoor community, Willsworthy, in 1932.

Let's go for a swim! Cornwall lads Roger, Nicholas and Peter Maxwell enjoy themselves at Polingey Mill in 1955.

Haughley Tennis Club's carnival float for the 1953 coronation celebrations.

Children of Mere in Wiltshire watch the hunt get ready.

Ivy, Ella, Jamie and Leslie Grigg show off their wonderful toy collection, about 1915, in Veryan, Cornwall.

A swimming party by the River Harbourne 1940s.

Celebrations at the dedication of the recast church bells in Carhampton, Somerset in 1929.

Above: *Do you remember metal pedal cars? Here, although aged about 7 and far too big for it, I am determined to pedal my pride and joy along the path in my Grandparents' back garden.*

Top right: *…but it wasn't just boys who had all the fun – this fine machine is being driven by Margaret Ann Rundle in Veryan and Portloe, around 1955.*

Right: *You can get two in this one! West Coker children Primrose, Peter and Dennis Clarke play in their car, 1935.*

School plays, trips, games and sports in the 1960s

Isabel MacLeod, Infants 1960s, recalled the following:

amazingly, worked. No bicycles, roller skates (if you were lucky enough to have them) were allowed on the premises.

1930s horrible dentist

Very occasionally we were examined by school doctors, dentists, eyesight and head-lice nurses. I did have to visit the school dentist in his surgery in South Norwood which was almost directly opposite the original Lady Edridge School to have a tooth removed using gas as an anaesthetic. It was the most awful experience of my young life. Although supposed to be unconscious, I felt the tooth being extracted and afterwards being barely awake was pulled out of the chair and led over to a sink, told to rinse, and in no time handed to my Mum. It was a most uncaring, unloving and heartless action. No wonder I have hated dentists every since.

In the top infants class I was in the Nativity play at Christmas as Mary, when I had to sing by myself. Being a rather serious and quiet child, I was not naturally a 'performer', but Miss Speller was very kind and made sure I did not take it too seriously and it all went well. I remember particularly the special make-up being put on: I had never worn any before, especially not bright red lipstick. Although why Mary had to wear bright red lipstick remains a mystery to me. That year there was also a visit to Chessington Zoo, where the main attraction even then was the ghost train and other amusements rather than animals. There was a hula hoop craze, with which I could not cope as I was not especially graceful. Maypole dancing was fun, however, and the maypole was moved about either in the hall or outside as required. We were encouraged to

A day off school for the thrilled children as Her Majesty Queen Elizabeth II visits Mere on 3 July 1952.

A beautiful beach scene at Blue Anchor which lies between the foothills of Exmoor and the Bristol Channel: a perfect day to take a trip around the bay.

'play' musical instruments, although I never progressed beyond the triangle. Music and movement meant listening to a radio programme for schools and interpreting the commands. Being a tree in the wind or whatever was always beyond me and, I thought, rather pointless… At the end of the summer term there were races, which were much more to my taste. The prizes for winners were cherries.

Junior department sports

Each summer I got involved with after-school athletics. This was organised by Mr Roberts who afterwards became my form teacher. He was helped by Mrs Ivy Clarke, a former dinner lady. We ran parallel to the railway line – 60 yards in the first year, 80 yards in the second and third years, culminating in 100 yards in the fourth year. We jumped into a sandpit situated on the Morland Road side beyond the 'new' building, always in my time occupied by third year classes. Mr Roberts had a box of assorted spiked running shoes to be borrowed. They were all black and if you were lucky you got a matching pair. Each year there was a trip to the Sports Arena in Albert Road for a practice before the Croydon Sports meeting. We walked there, ran a lot and then walked back to school again.

Funny bits 1930s

Clarice Kidd writes:

All the children had to do needlework, and one day I lost my needle. All through the lesson I pretended to sew. The teacher would have told me off if she had found out. I only told my Mum about it.

Pat Wiepen recalls:

During the war we had the playground dug up for a garden, and we all tended the vegetables and did the weeding – we all did something. One day some of the boys brought in snails from the garden. Bob Harrowven made us giggle as he brought them in tucked in his pocket. The teacher asked what we were laughing about. It was because he had put them into her needlework bag and they were all crawling out. She wasn't too pleased.

Sleeping at school

Thelma Kidd remembers staying overnight in school in wartime Norwich:

During the war our education took a tumble, and the

All smiles at the 1952 Christmas party at St Audries and West Quantoxhead, Somerset.

curriculum was followed. When the air raids took place on Norwich we often had a sleep at school. We collected waste-paper and cardboard – all we could lay our hands on – and stored it in the boys' cloakroom.

Pierrot shows and early cinema

Austin Toms, a former pilot, published a book in 1978, with Brenda Duxbury, called About Looe. This is not from this book, however, but from separate papers found afterwards:

I think it was before the First Wold War that we had a Pierrot party giving shows. A Mr Leonard, known by the nickname of 'Peggy' and his wife came and started this in Looe at the lower end of Church-end during the summer months. He built quite a respectable covered stage, between 20-25 ft long, with a small changing room at one side. There were footlights too, but how they were lit I couldn't say, and fencing around. The best seats were 20-30 deckchairs at 6d to 1 shilling for a performance. The rest of the seating consisted of wooden forms and cost 3d-6d I think.

During the show collecting boxes would go around, and

the show ended with a couple of short comic films. During the show Mr leonard's wife would sing two or three solos and act as pianist to the other performers. Sometimes the same artists would come back for two or three years in succession.

One comedian named Charlie Williams stayed for the duration of his life, and died about five years ago at the age of 81. He became a much respected citizen of the town, always willing to aid and put on a turn for any local charity. When his stage career ended he became a part-time postman but I think he ended up a full-time postman.

When Mr Leonard came to end his Pierrot show, for what reason I do not know, he took over what was now known as the public hall for a cinema and advertised it as the small-est cinema in England, seating around 150 the way he packed us in. The best two rows were where the stage was now, with five or six rows in front which were second best. The rest of the hall was filled with wooden forms and the lighting he generated himself. The noise at times could be deafening during an exciting cowboy and Indian film as his wife rattled away at the piano, as the films were all silent ones of course. Mr Leonard and his wife died in Looe several years ago.

Fancy a go at the cork game? Church fete in South Brent, 1950s.

A lovely bustling scene from Veryan Village, Cornwall, 1896. It features the round houses for which this village is remembered. Two boys appear to playing marbles while another is waiting for a game of cricket.

Whit Monday celebrations, the cricket match and evening fun and games
From *The Book of Wendling, Longham and Beeston with Bittering*

On Whit Monday the Band of Hope Annual fete (or treat, as it was called) was held in a meadow adjoining the barn. Wendling boasted a vigorous Band of Hope and this treat was a highly organised affair. To begin with, the Salvation Army from Dereham headed a long procession of blue ribboners who marched and sang around the village. Hale and hearty fellows were those bandsmen, particularly the drummer who, in the pauses between playing, would take off his red cap and wipe his perspiring head. It so happened that he had a particularly shiny bald head and, much to the amusement of his pals, one of the small boys called out: 'Coo look! Ole Harry 'a bin usin' metal polish'.

After the procession had returned to the meadow, an ambitious sports programme began. This included tug-of-war, pole-jumping, pillow-fighting on a greasy pole, and egg-and-spoon races for the children.

At one side of the field a cricket match was held between teetotallers and beer drinkers. The captain of the teetotallers was a tall and rather handsome young man called Fred Butcher. Bill Bradley was the beer drinkers' captain

(both on and off the field). These two wore cream shirts and trousers but most of the players were in their black Sunday suits, starched collars and bowler hats.

The beer drinkers won the toss and batted first. Bill Bradley took the first ball, which went miles wide of the stumps, beat the wicket-keeper all ends up and produced two easy runs. The next ball was a full toss, which Bill swiped into the field with a resounding smack. It sped towards the fieldsman head high, and smashed into the bowler hat of a short, fat youth of 20, named Charlie. A roar went up from the onlookers. 'Good ole Charlie. Keep yow yar hat on bor. You'll catch him out if he sends yow another like that there!' And so the game went on: full of fun and everyone in a good humour.

At the end of their innings, the beer drinkers had managed to knock up 56 runs and by this time tea was ready in the barn. Everyone in the village who could walk came to this tea. They sat on long wooden forms on either side of trestle tables covered with plates of ham sandwiches and fruit cake. The tea was free for all, provided out of the Band of Hope funds and, for the older folk, was the event of the day. There they would sit and talk about their rheumatics to their hearts' content. The children competed with one another in the number of sandwiches each could consume, dodging under the tables to avoid the restraining influence and admonishments of their parents.

Crudwell May Queen 1959.

Maypole dancing at Crudwell Court fete, around 1928.

When the tea was over, they rushed back to the meadow, most of them stealthily darting behind the bushes to prevent themselves from bursting with tea and lemonade. Games were resumed and the teetotallers began their innings on the cricket pitch. Five wickets fell for 14 runs and things looked bad. But at this stage Alfred Butcher and Maurice Carter made a stand, bringing the score to 38. Then the beer drinking bowler took off his hat and coat, rolled up his sleeves and called out: 'Yow've bin in there long enough together. I'm agoin' ter git one on yer out or I'll eart my hat'.

So saying, he walked back about 20 yards behind the wicket and, turning round, loped back again, gathering speed all the time. His hairy arm went over and, an instant later, so did Alfred's middle stump. It was soon all over after that and the honour of the beer drinkers was upheld by 13 runs.

By this time the evening shadows were extending from the towering elm trees and, over the little stream which wound its way along the far side of the meadow, a film of mist was rising, forecasting a fine day on the morrow. As soon as the sun had set there was a sudden swish like the hissing of escaping steam and, high above the heads of the happy crowd, a cluster of multi-coloured lights spread out like a gigantic fan. The firework display had begun. Children clapped their hands and danced with glee and old men stared with mouths wide open.

When the display was over, there were cries of 'Come on Willie Harbut … Gordie, thas time we wurra goin' hoom' and, one by one, the little family groups disappeared into the quietness of the night. For youths and maidens the fun was not yet over. Linking their hands together, they formed a circle and began the age-old game of kissing in the ring. Three girls and three boys started walking round the ring, the boys in one direction and the girls in the opposite. Each had a white handkerchief and dropped it onto the shoulder of a willing victim. Then began the chase. Girls ran giggling and screaming in all directions, each followed by an eager male. The first chase was a long one for as yet there was no competition. Each had chosen his or her favourite and the boys made sure that the girls reached the extremities of the meadow before they were caught. Then, with arms enfolded around each other, they kissed and sauntered back to the ring. From now on there was competition for the prettier girls and more handsome boys but, as time wore on, none was left out of the game.

The same book gives us a glimpse into the intensity of religious life in the village.

The May Queen of Lustleigh, Olive Chudley, on Dartmoor in 1906.

On Whit Sunday, the chapel held its school anniversary in a neighbouring barn. For weeks past the children had practised their songs and 'pieces', waiting impatiently for the day when they could put on their new suits and summer frocks and, standing in front of a platform made from sheep hurdles and wooden planks, display their knowledge of elocution.

Each year a favourite local preacher was invited to conduct the anniversary services. One year it was George Langdon, a huge, bearded man with beaming face and thunderous voice. He had walked some three or four miles from his little farmstead. On entering the barn , he removed his bowler hat. Wiping the sweat from his brow, he said how glad he was to be with his Wendling friends again and announced the first hymn. After the hymn, George knelt on the platform and prayed a long and ardent prayer and when he rose tears streamed down his face. For no good preacher could pray without emotion and the depth of his emotion was the standard by which he was judged.

Friendship 1920s and 30s – up to late 1950s

From *The Book of Stourton Caundle* by Philip Knott
'Down on bridge' by Frank Palmer

Until the late 1950s, the main meeting place for the children and young adults of the village was on the bridge, opposite the Trooper Inn. It was a common site to see men and children of all ages sat along the entire length of the bridge on a summer's evening. Everyone knew the place as 'down on bridge. 'Often there was not enough room for everyone to sit, and the younger children would hover between the groups of young adults present to listen to the conversation and adult humour. The topics of conversation never really changed: one's job of work, girls, risqué stories, local gossip and the catching of rabbits. There was always loud laughter, and we used to laugh along with the older men, even when we did not understand, or see the funny side of the story.

The younger children present also played various games in the street, until the arrival of the Police Constable from Stalbridge on his bicycle put a temporary halt to the proceedings. During the evening, with bedtime approaching for the younger children present, their mothers would arrive to collect them, hailing out from some distance to call them home, as they were too embarrassed to come too close for fear of some ribald comments from the young men congregated on the bridge. Football was also played in Ropers Field at the rear of the Trooper Inn. Men and boys of all age groups played until it was too dark to see the ball.

In the 1920s there were no wireless sets in the village, and on a Saturday evening, one young man would bring back an evening paper from Stalbridge, and all those present would eagerly gather around for the announcement of the results of the afternoon football matches. I can recall one man who attended the FA Cup final each year, and on Sunday he would give a ball by ball account of the match

Blofield Boy Scouts, 19 July 1919, with Canon Shillito in the garden of the rectory. Scouting thrived following the First World War.

Sport was one area where school and the wider community overlapped: here is the Lustleigh Colts Cricket team in 1948.

In a similar way, cubs, scouts, brownies and guides enhanced, and added to, skills learnt at school. This is a picture of Brown Owl, Mrs Taylor of Pimperne, and her Brownies 1962.

to those assembled on the bridge. The girls passing the bridge never seemed to object to the wolf whistles that came their way, and some of the married women would engage in a little banter. I can recall one who objected to the whistles calling out 'Go back to the farmyard where you belong'. There was so much natural spontaneous humour… I was frequently envious of the young men who owned a pedal cycle and who had a few shillings of spending money in their pockets. I used to consider them extremely wealthy, especially on the occasions they decided to leave the bridge, and cycle off to Sherborne to buy fish and chips, and in later years to attend the Picture Palace. Our village cyclists always risked a confrontation with the local police constable, due to the unreliability of either the oil, or carbide lamps on their bikes.

I fondly remember those many evenings, during the 1920s and 1930s, spent on the bridge. The humour and comradeship meant everything to us, but it really was harmless and innocent, just a bunch of local lads sitting on the bridge.

Mischevious looking Crudwell Cubs in 1954.

Below: *Many people assume that the idea of majorettes came over from America very recently: this wonderful picture, taken in 1976 at Crudwell fete, proves otherwise.*

Chapter Nine

What is That? School Food - the Good, the Bad and the Inedible

One should eat to live, and not live to eat.
MOLIERE
1622 - 1673

'Give me a child until he is seven, and I will give you the man'.
MODERN SAYING

Thus goes the saying about the child in his first seven years. Well, the same can be said for our food habits, I think: what we eat, or don't eat, as youngsters will influence our future tastes. On the *don't* front, I never had any exotic seafood like crab or lobster as a kid, or prawns or mussels and would find it very hard to eat them now.

Food at Hickstons

On the *do* front, I can vividly remember some meals from boarding school when I was six and seven. We had kippers on Friday for breakfast; ham and mashed potato every Sunday after church and tinned peaches and bread and butter for Sunday tea. I can recall a breakfast when I first had back bacon – the cook had run out of streaky and cooked this delicious and strange pink meat for us as a 'one off'. I was about seven. The other kids said things like ' Oh, just like home. Lovely'. I said the same but in truth had

When I was at school there were Mac Fisheries all over – I remember Mum would sometimes buy some fresh fish as a treat.

never tasted it before as times at home were a bit tough.

Breakfast was a bit of an occasion at Hickstons. The Reverend Quantock would eat standing up and walk around the breakfast room holding a radio and we all had to pay attention to the 8 o'clock BBC news. Then he would select a child to stand up and recite one of the news items: you would pray that, if you were selected, then you would be child number one or two as, if it got to item six or seven you were probably a gonner.

In our day schools, the provision of school meals was only recognised as a duty by Parliament in 1906. The country had been shocked by the state of the nation's young recruits who signed up for the Boer War in 1902. Mayhew's reports on the malnutrition in the inner cities of Edwardian times proved grim reading. The Provision of Meals Act was passed on the eve of war on August 4 1914. In the 1920s the provision of milk in schools became widespread. By the end of the second World War some third of children in Primary education received a meal at school, and free milk was made available in all grant-aided schools in 1946. The price of the meals increased from 6d in 1950 to 25p in 1977. The quality gradually became better, too: in the 1980s a concerted effort was made to reduce salt, fat and sugar in their production, a trend culminating in Jamie Oliver's recent campaigns for variety and freshness.

Pigs bellies, boiled eggs and cream

The Book of Haughley, by Haughley History Forum, gives an insight into how bad nutrition used to be.

149

George Clements, born in 1898, records:

We used to take home pigs' bellies, and do you know what, they used to scrape them and get two basins of lard, and then she (his mother) used to cut, not actually the pigs' belly, but sort of the outside, she used to cut off and make chiplets and put currants and sultanas with it and put them in a turnover. Oh by God we was bad off.

In *The Book of Peter Tavy with Cudlipptown,* by Peter Tavy Heritage Group, we hear that, before the First World War:

Food was not provided and after a breakfast of a boiled egg and a hunk of bread smothered with treacle and cream, Betty took sandwiches to school and crossed over the road to her aunt, Mrs Stratford at Jasmine Cottage, to eat them at lunchtime. The kitchen was not built until after the First World War when the authorities started bringing hot dinners to the school.

Cream figures large in the diet of some schoolchildren, particularly in Devon and Cornwall for obvious reasons. Some would go off across the fields to school fortified with bread and cream, homemade biscuit, cream and treacle or apple pie and cream. Apple pies were a staple food as no orchard was left with fruit when the trees were heavy. I remember fondly walks around the orchards and strawberry fields of Sutton Valence in Kent with my border collie, Boomer, in the 1990s when we would come across apples, some as big as footballs (really), left to rot in the fields: not so in days gone by as they would be gratefully collected and stored in the dark cupboard under the stairs for use in almost any variety of apple recipe in the next twelve months.

Cream-making was an art practised in many households, and we have a description of how to make it from Reg Bellamy in Postbridge. Although written in the 1970s, the recipe is ages old and quite authentic:

Making Devon Cream at home

My mother used this method for making cream until 1972. She and father used a separator for a short time but soon went back to the old ways.

The fresh milk, straight from the cow, was strained into a large enamelled pan and allowed to stand overnight. By morning the cream 'ream', as she called it, had risen to the top, and the pan was placed over some form of heat such as a Florence oilstove or a Rayburn.

The gentle heat allowed a 'scud' to form, which would be spoilt if the milk underneath boiled. The art was in knowing when to remove the pan from the heat and a good guide was when very small bubbles appeared on the 'scud'. After cooling the cream was removed from the milk using a 'reamer'.

This implement could be of several different shapes, each having a number of small holes allowing the milk to drain away. Each piece of cream was placed in a bowl, one on top of the other, until it was several inches thick. This is a sure way of identifying genuine Devonshire scalded cream. Over the years my mother must have made many hundredweights of cream using the scalded method. Much of what she made was posted all over the country.

The other great staple, if your family could afford it, was ham and bacon. You would, of course need to kill your pig first and preserve the meat:

The farmer's wife was busy in the farmhouse. At Treleigh at least two pigs were still being killed each year, to be cut up and preserved in the salter or salting keeve. This was an enormous granite trough in which the ham and bacon were placed between layers of salt, for one month. Then the surplus salt was wiped off, the meat wrapped first in newspaper, then in an old flour sack with a bit of hay inside, and hung – bacon on bacon rack, hams all around the walls, where they could dry out in the warmth rising from the cooker range. Nothing was wasted. The tripe was taken down the river and washed clean. At Treleigh three men were employed permanently, but at harvest time casuals, known as 'slingers', were needed to help and the pig meat was needed to feed the extra workers.

Source: *The Book of St Ervan* by Moira Tangye

Some early suggestions for nutritious eating

It took a long time for government policy to really 'get a grip' on the nutrition of school food. As ever in the history of our islands, it was often left to well-intentioned voluntary efforts to provide solutions. Public libraries have many collections of 'instructions' for the feeding of the poorer classes. One of particular interest is a very early manual by Charles Elme Francatelli who was, for a time, no less than the Chief Cook to Queen Victoria. It has recently been re-issued and makes fascinating reading. One thing he suggests for breakfast is 'Thick Milk' comprising milk, into which has been stirred a tablespoon of flour for each pint. It should be heated for ten minutes, seasoned with a little salt and served with bread or a boiled potato. It is hard to imagine a modern child, rushing to school, abandoning his cocoa-flavoured flakes or star-shaped corn pops in favour of this bland concoction. Another suggestion is a porridge made of milk, onions and oatmeal, again seasoned with salt: sugar was a rare commodity in those days. On the way home, 'industrious and intelligent' boys could catch maybe a dozen small birds, pluck them, remove their heads, claws and gizzards and present them to Mum who could make a 'famous pudding'. I am sure Mum was delighted - but how times change!

Another thing this book helped me with was 'Toast Water'. I have always wondered why, when anyone is sick in Charles Dickens' novels, they are put to bed and fed 'Toast Water'. Well, it is apparently exactly what it seems – toast (not burnt) mixed with hot water. A lot of his characters tend to expire quite quickly. Hmm…

There are, too, many dozens of school meals booklets produced by volunteers and voluntary societies of many kinds. One thing that strikes the modern reader, particularly by those produced between the wars, is that they may have been filling but were not healthy by our reckoning. A typical recipe would probably contain a lot of cheese, batter and fatty gravy and be served with bread.

The diet of secondary schoolchildren has, since the early 19th century, been supplemented by items bought in the 'tuck shop'. The tuck shop in my school sold principally, crisps, chocolate and fizzy drinks. 'Tuck' is slang for 'food' and tuck shops can be found in schools throughout the former Empire. They may have originated in my home city of Norwich where there used to be the celebrated 'Tuck's Coffee House' in the wonderfully named 'Gentleman's Walk' – where gentleman would parade up and down in their best finery, dropping into the coffee shops along the way now and again for conversation and reading. 'Tucks Coffee House' had on sale a tempting selection of goodies to eat as well as a library for patrons' use.

As late as the 1930s, many children attended school both cold and hungry. Miss Lee, a concerned Headmistress featured in *The Book of Honiton* at that time remarked: ' *These children should not have to come to school so cold and tired, we cannot expect them to learn'.* One of her charges, Margaret Robson, remembers: ' *Many children came hungry, too; I took bread and butter and banana sandwiches for years. I suppose bananas were* cheap and in any case very nourishing. I thought I was a cut above the children who brought bread with no butter and an apple, but below those who brought chicken sandwiches wrapped in greaseproof paper'.*

Cyril Skerrett started school at this period. He says:

Mrs Jones had been replaced by Mrs Prowse as headteacher with another teacher in the small room where the infants started. The same coke stove heated the big room and water was still brought in from the pump outside. Mrs Prowse would boil eggs brought by the children or heat up their pasties for lunch. She would make us a cup of cocoa for a charge of only a halfpenny a week.

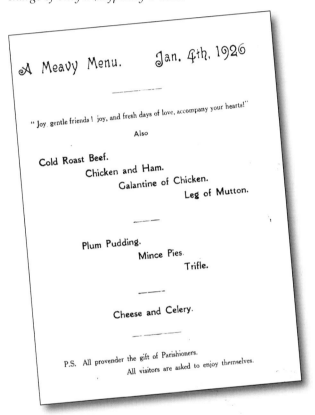

A special celebratory school menu from 1926, Meavy, Dartmoor.

Not everyone was so badly off. Eric John Vine, born 1937, recalls:

I have lived in various houses in the same area all my life. I went to Leigh Hurst School. It had three classrooms, but there were four classes run by three teachers. Mr Owen G Davies, the headmaster, taught two classes in one room. He taught English, geography, gardening – everything!

We had meals in the classrooms, which were prepared in the Memorial Hall by local ladies. They also provided the meals for the Leigh Sinton School. The meals cost 2s1d

1995 and Shirley Stamp serves up her last Christmas lunch at Honiton Community College, Devon.

Children tucking in at the St Mary Magdalene Oval Road Sunday School, Addiscombe, near Croydon, 1943.

(11p) per week, and they were beautiful.. There was a main course, with lots of variety, and a pudding. The lady in charge of preparing meals was Mrs Drew, who lived in Post Office Lane, Bransford, and my mother, Ethel Vine, helped to cook.

We ate at our desks. The sloping tops were propped up to make them level by a peg inside the desk. Two desks were put together and a cloth put over them, and the dinner ladies put out the cutlery.

My memories of school food

My memories of school meals date mainly from secondary school days. As we were boarders we ate separately from the day boys but I think the meals were pretty much of a muchness. We sat six boys to a table, the most senior boys at one end of the hall and the youngest at the other. The senior boys were given their food first – always in large bowls so that everyone got to serve themselves. This meant two things – first, if chief cook, Betty, a much-loved lady who unfortunately hardly knew one end of a carrot from another – doled out too much to the senior boys, then the junior ones got bowls with less and less in them; secondly, if you were last at the table to serve yourself from the bowl, you might find that there was not much left in it.

I have vivid memories of my first breakfast when, with five of my little colleagues, I was sitting at the most junior end of the hall. The conversation was all about Dads – everyone but me seemed to have a Dad that was at least a cabinet minister or chief advisor to the Queen or some other fantastical thing – mine ran a restaurant on the seafront at Weston-super-Mare. Each boy took it in turns to tell their tale and I remember waiting with dread for my turn to come. As they talked, the bowl came round and each helped himself. I was spared my ordeal because, being the last to help myself from the bowl, all the others were tucking in by the time my turn to speak had come. Unfortunately, all that was left in the bowl were a few baked beans and half a runny egg, and it looked disgusting. Up to this day, I have never been able to eat any meal that comprises both egg and baked beans. I was reciting this recently to a neighbour of mine about the same age as me and was most surprised to learn that he suffers from the same 'condition' for much the same reasons.

A children's tea party in Haughley, Suffolk, in 1945 – it seems to be just what it says, a tea party as there does not appear to be any food around!

A children's Christmas party in Mulbarton, near Norwich, Norfolk in the 1950s.

Dinner ladies were often much-loved – here, children of the Old School, Easton, Norfolk say goodbye to Maggie Mortimer, the dinner lady, around 1970.

In a very unscientific survey I have been asking people about their favourite schoolday meals from the 50s, 60s and 70s. It is amazing how similar they all are. The following were mentioned often:

> Cheese flan
> Toad-in-the-hole (with burnt edges)
> Spam fritters and tinned tomatoes
> Sausage and mash
> Liver and onions with cabbage
>
> Jam tart
> Spotted dick
> Tapioca/rice/semolina with jam
> Prunes
> Banana custard

It is interesting that, today, memories of school meals are mostly very affectionate. Indeed, there are clubs in big cities dedicated to recreating the classics.

Concerning Pies

I have always liked pies. Every Wednesday lunchtime we would get these luke-warm, oblong, flattish, grey, damp, floppy, pastry things which Betty, our chief cook, told us were 'meat' pies – absolutely not 'beef' or 'chicken' or 'pork' floppy, pastry things, but 'meat' floppy, pastry things. Thinking back now, I hate to imagine what was in them, and it took me many years to work out that 'meat' did not mean vaguely acrid-tasting lumps of fat along with some challenging pieces of gristle to give your teeth some exercise. If you took the top off, you could see the 'meat' stuck to the bottom pastry layer by a brown sticky dampness. They were immeasurably disgusting but I had a soft spot for them. Their modern-day counterparts can be found in the cheapest supermarkets in the 'gravy and steak' pie section: many times I have found my hand wandering towards them until my rational brain issues the command 'pull yourself together!'

A special word about liver

A special word must be said about liver. It seems that all liver came with lots of veins and was always over-cooked. Here is a spoof schooldays liver recipe from someone who wishes to remain anonymous:

Take cheapest liver. Cook in oven for specified time. Repeat. Take each piece and burn edges under grill.

Take bright green cabbage. Boil until a pale yellow colour and it smells like the inside of a compost bin. Drain, but not too well, as each dollop must be served in a sea of water.

Take pan of fat that has been hanging around kitchen, heat, and add flour and gravy browning. Care should be taken to create lots of lumps.

Serve on cold plates.

I admit to being so hungry that I always ate my liver. Not so, everyone, it seems. David Wootton, of the hugely popular Maggie Secker programme on BBC Radio Norfolk, had a more radical solution: 'I put it in my blazer pocket'. But then, he went to a posh school and they did things like that.

One great advantage of residing in Beckenham is the availability of a Fresh

MILK SUPPLY

"The Best for Baby."

W. J. HERBERT

1 THESIGER ROAD, SYDENHAM. Syd. 6334
3 EDEN PARADE, BECKENHAM
GUERNSEY DAIRY, DOWNE
and 111 HIGH STREET, PENGE

Sells only Milk in the same condition as given by the cow with all its rich qualities, and from Local Farms accredited by the Milk Marketing Board. Delivered to you in sealed bottles within one hour of milking

One of the Oldest Established Dairies in Beckenham

For several decades in the early 20th century, milk was seen as the key for healthy growth in babies and schoolchildren.

Chapter Ten

Schooldays in the Arts
pop music, plays, films and literature

Dylan talked copiously, then stopped. 'Somebody's boring me,' he said, 'I think it's me.'
RAYNER HEPPENSTALL, FOUR ABSENTEES (1960)

Please, sir, he's weeding the garden," replied a small voice. To be sure,"
said Squeers, by no means disconcerted. "So he is. B-o-t, bot, t-i-n, tin, bottin,
n-e-y, ney, bottinney, noun substantive, a knowledge of plants. When he has
learned that bottinney means a knowledge of plants, he goes and
knows 'em. That's our system, Nickleby; what do you think of it?"

Nicholas Nickleby
CHARLES DICKENS

Get me out of here

'I don't like Mondays!' sang the Boomtown Rats. Alice Cooper let us celebrate that 'School's out for Summer' while Itchycoo Park promised the hidden delights of 'getting high'. What these pop songs have in common is that they were not about being in school itself but of *getting out* of the place. Just before these sixties and seventies hits we had the gentler sounds of the 1950s but, even then, kids did not want to hear about classrooms but of taking a pretty girl to the High School Prom or of girls and boys taking their love into a land beyond the school gates. Probably, pop music was then too impatient a medium to explore the complexities of life for boys and girls – after all, you only had three minutes to make your statement.

Not that pop music was not one of the most important aspects of schooldays: quite the reverse. It helped define you to your mates. In my grammar school in the sixties you could be a Beatles fan – nice, tuneful, respectful and with a hint of rebelliousness; you could like the Rolling Stones – much more hard edged, you could wear your hair a bit long and, if you cheeked teachers then that was good for you street cred; or you could try to be more interesting and play the Who, as my friend, Pete did, and support unfashionable causes; and then, if you really wished to go out on a limb for the sheer hell of it, you could get into jazz. But such things were seen as defining you as a human being, not academically.

Until the advent of the Harry Potter movies, which completely turned things on their head, films and plays about schooldays were surprisingly rare. It was just so uncool. Great decade-defining films like Kubrick's 'A Clockwork Orange' were about the complete opposite – telling the adults to 'go hang' and deliberately breaking moral taboos, to a shocking degree. Anderson's 'If' was all about rebellion and blowing up the school. As regards plays, until recently with Alan Bennett's magnificent 'History Boys' which engagingly considers school themes like sexuality, friendship and the nature of success, the picture was similar.

The written word

Where schoolday experience has been explored very successfully for several hundred years, however, is in books and stories. In 1749 Sarah Fielding wrote *The Governess or The Little Female Academy* which explored friendship and morality in – remarkable for the time given the paucity of female educational opportunities – a girls' school. This set the standard for the genre. Many school stories were published thereafter leading to the 'golden age' of novels in the 1800s, where young people featured in truly great novels. In 1857, *Tom Brown's Schooldays* by Thomas Hughes took Britain, and thus the world as it was then, by storm. This was, of course, at about the same time that Charles Dickens was writing *Dombey and Son*, *David Copperfield* and *Nicholas Nickelby* and, to my mind, is equally great. Thomas Hughes wrote more books but none were to reach the visceral realism of this one. He was, not unkindly meant, a sort of one and a half hit wonder, but given the supreme artistry of *Tom Brown's Schooldays*, who would not swap places with him? After all, Arthur Conan Doyle was the same,

This Earthly World

You tell me I am getting old, but that's not really so.
The house I live in may be worn and that of course I know,
It's been in use a good long while and weathered many a gale,
I'm therefore not surprised to find it's getting somewhat frail.

You tell me I am getting old, you mix my house with me,
You're looking at the outside, that's all that most folk see,
The dweller in the little house is young and bright and gay,
Just starting on a life that lasts through long eternal day.

The colour changing of the roof, the windows getting dim,
The walls a bit transparent and getting rather thin,
The foundations not so steady as once they used to be
And that is all that you observe, but it is not really me.

I patch the old house up a bit to make it last the night
But soon I shall be flitting to my home of endless light.
I'm going to live for ever there, my life goes on, it's grand.
How can you say I'm getting old? You do not understand.

These few short years can't make me old, I feel I'm in my youth,
Eternity lies just ahead, full life and joy and truth.
We will not fret to see this house grow shally day by day,
But look ahead to our new home which never will decay.

I want to be made fit to dwell in that blest house above,
Cleansed in the precious blood of Christ and growing still in love.
The beauty of that glorious home, no words can ever say,
'Tis hid from our mortal eyes, but kept for us some day.

My House is getting ready in the land beyond the sky,
Its architect and builder is my Saviour now on high,
But I rather think He's leaving the furnishing to me,
So it's 'treasure up in heaven' I must store each day, you see.

This lovely poem, written by Revd Austin Lester, rector of Peter Tavy on Dartmoor 1908-32, just before he died in 1949 has, I feel, an eternal youthfulness about it and feels suitable for the subject matter of these pages.

just dashing off the Sherlock Holmes stories because he had no clients coming to his eye surgery, and struggling to write what he thought of as greater literature for the rest of his life. The public was not really interested. Some people hit the bulls-eye and are bemused by how they did it.

The genre is very difficult. One who must have lived to regret writing a schoolday novel at all was Dean Farrar, author of *Eric, or Little by Little*, published in 1858. It is funny for all the wrong reasons. Boys address each other like statesmen in Parliament, about love, honour and loyalty. Boys don't talk like that! Farrar, something of a firebrand preacher, charts the moral decline and eventual death of a boy who only seeks God's repentance on his deathbed. Boys come across as pretty nasty creatures and the downward spiral of the 'hero' is saturated with melodrama and sentimentality, not least in the almost constant death scenes. Dickens could (only) just get away with melodrama of this type, being infinitely more skilled as a writer. I was often reminded, when reading the book, of Oscar Wilde's cruel but brilliant jibe which actually refers to the death of Little Nell in Dickens' *The Old Curiosity Shop* – 'you would have to have a heart of stone not to laugh'. As a review of 1858 said 'everything is served up with tear sauce'. But then, the Victorians loved this kind of thing and the book went through 36 editions in Farrar's own lifetime.

The complete opposite is to be found in *Prelude*, a novel written by Beverley Nicholas and published in 1920. It contains a lovely passage about friendship:

There is nothing in the world more sacred or more beautiful than the love of a boy for his friend. In that love there was no element of the physical. It is true that Paul loved his friend's face, he loved the distinguishing touch of diablerie that showed itself from time to time, but that was all. He felt that without him life would be a blank. If he wasn't there, who would there be to tell that the moon was a crescent of silver over the roofs of the Lea House? Who would there be to show his latest poems? To whom could he tell the latest scandals about Ma Baker, to whom would he tell the little stories of his life which he told to nobody else? And whose arm would he link in his when prep was done and walk slowly and silently over to the classroom for prayers? No, he could never believe that he and Jack would not be together till the end of their lives; he dreamed of new

fields to explore; he saw then going hand in hand to see what it was that lay behind the clouds on the hills.

Paul whistled softly to himself. His eyes opened wide and then half closed with thought. How funny it all was, how damned funny! He laughed out loud.

Jack looked up and smiled. 'What the deuce is the matter?' he said.

Paul flushed slightly; he was not prepared to answer. 'Oh, nothing,' he said, yet with a wide but strange smile on his lips.

'I believe it's something shady, or you wouldn't go so purple in the face over it,' said Jack cynically, and went on with his book. Paul tried to cultivate this idea, it was faintly flattering to him; but his mind fell back and became once more introspective. How calm and rich and splendid everything seemed tonight. Here he was, aged 16, sitting in the best beloved place in the world, next to the best beloved friend that man had ever had. Here was the cup at his very lips, full to overflowing, let him drink it to the dregs. But he knew that not till he had left would he realise the full glory of those days. He thought of Cecil's lines:

'And earth has taught us in ole days our might,
Shooting dim glory, field and darkening lane
And crackling woods where rocks scream loud with fright,
And bare wet rolling downlands after rain.'

How wonderful life was!'

In my opinion, the most perfect novel – not the greatest – ever written is *A Christmas Carol* by Charles Dickens. It is short and there is not a word out of place. It is about kindness and education. In tone it sums up an era. Tiny Tim is a fine symbol, – especially for these pages. He is vulnerable and yet has beauty denied his more worldy-wise contemporaries. He can die, given harsh treatment, or he can live to inspire us all, given a smidgen of generosity. Mercifully, Scrooge is converted and becomes a 'second father' to him. Or does Tiny Tim become a second father to Scrooge?

Let the last words be, fittingly, from Tiny Tim:

'God Bless Us, Every One!'

WHEN SCHOOLDAYS WERE FUN

WHEN SCHOOLDAYS WERE FUN